Hidc

MW01257917

"This mindful practice of prayer-walking is a powerful way to notice the beauty of creation around us, to put our own struggles into perspective, to see needs for prayer around us, and to allow God's peace to settle over our souls. The practice healed me from depression and irrational fears, so I encourage you to read this lovely book."

—**Janet Holm McHenry,** national speaker and author of 24 books, including the best-selling *PrayerWalk* and her newest, *The Complete Guide to the Prayers of Jesus*

"This book is an invitation to slow our rhythms, disengage from the hurried pace of our everyday spaces, and connect with God in the cathedral of his created world. Sarah's inspired words replenished my spirit and reminded me of the power of stepping into nature and leaning into the Creator's love. This book reads like a poem and a prayer. I'll be returning to this book as a source of spiritual nourishment for years to come."

—**Stacey Pardoe,** author of *Flourish in the Fire* and *Mornings with Jesus*; founder of Encountering God in the Ordinary

"Each short chapter is a vivid word picture of God's provision and goodness. These images will stay with me, serving as prayer prompts. I loved this book for its simple yet evocative descriptions and relatable stories, and I believe it will create a lasting and positive impact to deepen my prayer life."

—**Dawn Klinge,** author of the Historic Hotels Collection: *Sorrento Girl, Biltmore Girl,* and *Palmer Girl*

"With her dog's leash in hand and a gravel road underfoot, Sarah Geringer grounds her readers in the concrete and the physical—then transports us to the world of the Spirit. With refreshing candor, this book applies biblical truth to the harsh realities of life on broken ground. The nodding heads of daffodils, the bitter Missouri wind, and the liquid trill of bird song nourish the soul, for they are God's provision."

—**Michele Morin,** Bible teacher, writer, and gardener who blogs at *Living Our Days*

"This is a soul-awakening invitation to a new kind of prayer life. It inspires you to step outside with God, encountering the Father-Creator in his glorious creation. Then it changes you as you reflect on your heart, thought patterns, and character. Sarah's reflections give fresh meaning to the phrase 'my walk with God,' reminding us of the joys that await us when we *walk* with God."

—**Elizabeth Laing Thompson,** author of *All the Feels, All the Feels for Teens,* and the When God Says series

"This book is a gift to anyone trying to find God's presence in the middle of life. Many people struggle with prayer and spending time with God, but Sarah invited people into an experience that is both practical and beautiful, simple and powerful, normal and holy."

—**Rev. Brett Cheek,** Teaching Pastor, La Croix Church

"Sarah's latest devotional invites readers to travel along with her on quietly introspective walks of faith, journeying down country lanes and woodland paths with her faithful, four-legged friend, Memphis, by her side. Vulnerable, raw, reflective, honest, and inspiring, *Hidden Manna on a Country Road* is not to be missed by anyone seeking a closer walk with God."

—**Tama Fortner,** ECPA award-winning and best-selling author

"This book brings the majesty, peace, and lessons from God's natural world into your home via insights shared through masterful storytelling. We too often find ourselves wandering in the wilderness of this world. Knowing that God's hidden manna is out there awaiting our discovery makes every next step in this journey an adventure. It is on those country roads of our lives that God invites us into quiet moments of reflection and prayer with him alone. It is in those moments that his manna is most often found."

—**J. D. Wininger,** writer and speaker at jdwininger.com

"In this tenderly vulnerable book, Sarah recounts her walks with God along the generational Midwestern landscape of her home. In these pages you'll find beautiful prayers penned from Sarah's heart and relevant reminders of God's intimate presence throughout the seasons of our lives. Join Sarah and her dog Memphis as they walk alongside you in this book, and discover afresh the sweet manna of God's presence hidden amidst everyday life."

—**Brenda Bradford Ottinger,** writer of Encouragement for Today devotions for Proverbs 31 Ministries

"Sarah Geringer is inviting us into the journey of prayer-walking. We do well to accept the invitation as she draws us into the sights, sounds, and seasons of a country road to hear nothing less than the still, small voice of God."

—**Travis Scholl,** author of *Walking the Labyrinth*

"Taking us through physical, emotional, and spiritual seasons on her daily prayer walks, Sarah describes the outer and inner landscape of her life to encourage us to get outside and look and listen for God's hidden manna in our lives. Read Sarah's journey with God and embark on your own."

—**Eugene C. Scott,** writer at eugenecscott.com, poet, outdoorsman, and pastor at Saint James Presbyterian Church, Littleton, CO

HIDDEN MANNA
on a
Country Road

Sarah Geringer

HIDDEN MANNA

on a
Country Road

Seeing God's Daily Provision All around Us

SARAH GERINGER

LEAFWOOD
PUBLISHERS
an imprint of Abilene Christian University Press

HIDDEN MANNA ON A COUNTRY ROAD
Seeing God's Daily Provision All around Us

L E A F W O O D
P U B L I S H E R S
an imprint of Abilene Christian University Press

Copyright © 2022 by Sarah Geringer

ISBN 978-1-68426-102-4 | LCCN 2022017716

Printed in the United States of America

Published in association with WordWise Media Services.

LIBRARY OF CONGRESS CATALOGING-IN-PUBLICATION DATA
Names: Geringer, Sarah, 1977- author.
Title: Hidden manna on a country road : seeing God's daily provision all around us / by Sarah Geringer.
Description: Abilene, Texas : Leafwood Publishers, [2022]
Identifiers: LCCN 2022017716 (print) | LCCN 2022017717 (ebook) | ISBN 9781684261024 | ISBN 9781684268931 (kindle edition)
Subjects: LCSH: Nature—Religious aspects—Christianity—Prayers and devotions. | Prayer—Christianity—Miscellanea. | Spiritual life—Christianity—Prayers and devotions. | Spirituality—Christianity—Prayers and devotions.
Classification: LCC BR115.N3 G47 2022 (print) | LCC BR115.N3 (ebook) | DDC 242—dc23/eng/20220526
LC record available at https://lccn.loc.gov/2022017716
LC ebook record available at https://lccn.loc.gov/2022017717

Cover design by Greg Jackson, ThinkPen Design | Interior text design by Sandy Armstrong, Strong Design

Leafwood Publishers is an imprint of Abilene Christian University Press
ACU Box 29138 | Abilene, Texas 79699

1-877-816-4455 | www.leafwoodpublishers.com

22 23 24 25 26 27 28 / 7 6 5 4 3 2 1

In honor of Memphis,
my loyal companion.

CONTENTS

SUMMER

AUTUMN

ACKNOWLEDGMENTS

I thank the Lord God Almighty for working all things together for me to write this book. You planted the love for this area in my heart as a little girl. You gave me the dreams to write as a teenager. You secured this property for me as a young woman, and you have been faithful to allow me to steward my beloved little corner of southeast Missouri. I treasure this region of your world, and it brings me abundant joy to introduce it to others through this book.

I thank my children, Drake, Ethan, and Lauren, for supporting me in my writing. You know how incredibly difficult this journey has been, and the spiritual warfare I face for doing God's will affects you too. But you three are the greatest blessings I've ever received, and I'm so thankful to see God's light shining in each of you.

I am deeply thankful for my faithful tribe of email and social media supporters. You have carried me through very hard seasons with your prayers and gifts of support. I could not have produced this book without your intercessory prayers and encouragement. You are a joy to serve.

Thank you to my agent, Michelle Lazurek, and the team at Leafwood Publishers, particularly Jason Fikes and Duane Anderson. Working with you has never felt like work—it's been such a gift! I appreciate your vision and guidance, which has made each of my books much better for a wider audience.

Finally, thank you to my readers. It's a pleasure to write for you and hear from you!

Soli Deo Gloria

INTRODUCTION

Whoever has ears, let them hear what the Spirit
says to the churches. To the one who is victorious, I
will give some of the hidden manna. I will also give
that person a white stone with a new name written
on it, known only to the one who receives it.

Revelation 2:17 NIV

"Father God, help me," I cried out in the bitter November wind with
a shaky voice. Our rocky marriage of nineteen years at the time
was at its lowest point. In a fit of anger, my husband had consulted
with a divorce attorney instead of visiting a marriage counselor
like I had requested. He had threatened to remove his wedding
ring and refused to celebrate our autumn anniversary with normal
fanfare. Tears nearly froze on my face as I walked north on the
gravel road, seeking God's presence in my heartache.

With each step, I poured out a vulnerable mixture of emotions
in prayer. Fear. Anger. Worry. Hurt. As a child of divorce, I knew
full well the nuclear fallout of my parents' choices, and I did not
want that for our three children. The barren landscape matched
my weary spirit, spent of all hope.

13

The fields were falling asleep in late fall. Grasses had turned brown and brittle. Hills were gray in the evening light. Surveying them, I imagined our marriage dying after many years of struggles. The grief inside my heart seemed too great to bear, although I knew God was right beside me.

Then I came upon a spot where I knew daffodils bloomed every single spring. Their bulbs were now buried under piles of dead leaves. Yet I could count on their yellow faces to cheer me next March, surely as I could count on the sun rising the next morning. That November, a hopeful rebloom of my marriage seemed impossible. But on that gravel road, I dried my tears as I remembered God's promise:

> Because of the Lord's great love we are not consumed,
>   for his compassions never fail.
> They are new every morning;
>   great is your faithfulness. (Lam. 3:22–23 niv)

Indeed, that fact about God's faithfulness, revealed to me on my prayer walk, held true the following spring. I saw it in the nodding heads of the daffodils on cool spring mornings, and I thanked God for the unexpected hope I had found in him alone. Though our marriage eventually fell apart two years later, I fiercely clung to the hope I found on prayer walks where God had communed with me so many times. The spring daffodils will always be a reminder of the hope God has tucked away for me in nature signs on my country road.

I have long been a praying woman, nature lover, walking enthusiast, and joy seeker. But I did not connect all these qualities until I started prayer walking in 2019, a full fifteen years after inhabiting this little portion of Missouri where my family first settled four generations ago. On two country roads, I found more hidden joys in both the physical and spiritual world than ever before. Special sessions with God became more frequent on my prayer walks than in any other place, and they filled me with joy during three tough years of my life.

Since the mid-1990s, I've kept a perpetual calendar with calligraphic names of God. I resurrected this calendar from my personal treasure trove in 2020, when I needed daily reminders of God's unchanging character in the chaos of our cultural shift. In May, I was intrigued by a name culled from Revelation 2:17: *hidden manna*. God as hidden manna? Curious, I pulled out my Bible to learn more.

In this section of Revelation, God was speaking to the church of Pergamum. He praised them for being true to his name, yet he chastised some church members for following false teachings. God invited them to repent and promised to give some of the hidden manna to those who were victorious. But where was this hidden manna?

I had to flip back to Exodus 16 to retrace the original appearance of manna. It was a gift God gave the Israelites while they were wandering in the wilderness. This bread from heaven sustained them in a land that could scarcely be cultivated for food. The Israelites were instructed to gather it in the morning, collecting only what they needed for the day. They gathered a double portion the day before the Sabbath so they could honor God's directive to rest one day of the week. If they gathered more than they needed, it quickly spoiled.

This manna was a physical manifestation of God's provision and loving care. He instructed Moses to place a measure of it inside the Ark of the Covenant, alongside the tablets that bore the Ten Commandments, as a reminder to future generations (Exod. 16:34). That which rotted in less than twenty-four hours was supernaturally preserved in this hidden jar under the shade of the mercy seat, kept in the Holy of Holies, where the high priest would make an atonement sacrifice once a year for the sins of the people (Lev. 16). All this was a foreshadowing of Jesus's once-and-for-all sacrifice for believers to come, including you and me.

Why would God reveal a vision including hidden manna to the apostle John, thousands of years after manna first appeared in the wilderness? Was manna a reward for true faith? I believe the hidden manna in Revelation was as much a symbol of God's provision and loving presence then as it is now, for us in the twenty-first century. Although we do not have the Ark of the Covenant anymore, nor the temple where sacrifices were made in Jesus's day, we have hidden manna tucked all around us, including signs of God's provision and loving care and proof that he will give us victory if we are wholeheartedly committed to him in these changing times.

In the spring of 2019, our family adopted a Labrador retriever puppy we named Memphis, who forced me to take daily walks on our county roads in southeast Missouri. Although I have lived on this particular property since 2004, I had not explored the roads on foot until my dog pulled me outside. I started dedicating my daily walks as times for prayer. Soon, I was amazed at the prayer prompts I found in ordinary things on my walk—hidden manna, if you will; beautiful reminders of God's presence and provision, right outside my door, reminders I had missed for years while driving these roads in my vehicle, but tangible and delightful once I slowed down to notice them on foot. They were sweet to my soul, like freshly baked bread from heaven.

Many Christians feel confused, overwhelmed, and guilty about their prayer lives. They want to connect with God, but they fear they are doing it wrong. They also want to slow down and disconnect from the frantic pace of our technology-driven world. If you feel this way, I understand. It took my 125-pound Labrador retriever's insistence on daily exercise to help me slow my pace, develop a daily prayer rhythm, and connect with God in nature.

I found dozens of connection points, aka hidden jars of manna, on my walks. They were simple and uncomplicated, and each enriched my relationship with God.

I pray that by describing my journey of prayer walking, your eyes will open to the manna sprinkled right outside your door, which is food for a profoundly meaningful connection with God. May my array of forty forms of hidden manna send you on a prayer expedition and manna collection in your part of this world.

In Christ's love,

Sarah Geringer

WINTER

CHAPTER ONE

NO SERVICE

And you are living stones that God is building into
his spiritual temple. What's more, you are his holy
priests. Through the mediation of Jesus Christ,
you offer spiritual sacrifices that please God.

1 Peter 2:5 NLT

When I started walking these country roads, I chose to leave my phone at home. The cell service is terrible here. The closest tower is still on a 3G network, so the Internet connection is as slow as molasses. I cannot receive or place calls, so what's the point of taking my phone along? I also wanted a distraction-free environment in which I did not have to worry about Big Tech subversively listening in on my verbal prayers. Besides, if my family needed me, they knew I was less than ten minutes away on foot and less than two minutes away by car.

Memphis and I headed out only with a leash. I soon realized the beauty of no service is living in the moment, in getting away from technology and submerging myself in nature. This is the first step of my prayer walk liturgy—quiet reverence, worship by observation.

I start the times of prayer in mindful silence, listening only to the sounds around me, a surprising cacophony, even in winter: crunching gravel beneath my feet; twigs snapping under Memphis's paws, his claws clicking on the asphalt; wind rustling through the trees, rattling through the few reddish-brown leaves still clinging high on the branches of the white oak. When we diverge onto the lawn, wading through a sea of dead leaves, I hear loud, crashing, sweeping sounds like ocean waves. Tuning in near the levee, I listen to the juncos, titmice, and cardinals picking through tufts of grass for seeds and a muffled ruffling when they stop to fluff their feathers for warmth; squirrels alighting on leaves, scurrying up tree bark, and bouncing across branches; and the howling northern wind itself, deftly weaving through grasses left uncut on the roadsides—a symphony of praise to begin the liturgical service.

This introduction, populated only by sounds of nature, settles me into worship mode. If I listen carefully enough, I can hear my own heartbeat keeping time when I press my gloved finger up to my hooded and scarf-wrapped ear. I hear my own breath pushing back and forth in a varying rhythm through my scarf. The manna of sound, all around and even within me, is a call to worship. These are sounds I would most certainly miss if I traveled the exact same path in my car with heated seats, my cold thighs remind me. But as I switch my gloved hands—one inside my pocket for greater warmth, one holding the leash—I remind myself: if I miss the sounds, I miss the worship manna.

The service begins. This jubilation of nature moves me to praise God first. Then the liturgy shifts to confession. I repeat the memorized prayer I learned as a Lutheran schoolgirl, a prayer that reminds me that I am a sinner by nature and deserve only punishment. But because Jesus died in my place, I have blessed salvation from my daily sins. He will renew me as I walk in his ways, because I am created to glorify him. This prayer cleanses me as I walk down the wooded hill toward the open gravel road.

Then I mull on the truths from my morning One Year Bible reading, which includes teachings from the Old Testament and the New Testament Epistles. I am already positioned upright for the reception of the gospel. My heart is singing a sermon hymn as I turn onto the short, backwards-J-shaped gravel road. Facing due north, bracing myself against the bitter wind, I dig into the meat of my prayer requests, as the sermon is the main course of a liturgical service. I wrestle with God in these matters, just like I fight against the cold wind.

After laying the matters before God, I praise him as I offer them before his throne. Then I turn south with the wind at my back. It is time to intercede for others. I pray for them by name, one by one, their faces appearing before me in my mind, although my focus is on the road, trees, fields, and sky. I end with a song of praise as I ascend the hill homeward. The same benediction in Numbers 6:24–26 that has been spoken over me thousands of times in corporate worship seems a fitting end for my intercessory prayers—may you shine your face on them, Lord, and give them your peace.

I am thankful there is no cell phone service on my prayer walk. I feast on the manna of silence, the manna of nature as I worship God through prayer. I partake in this liturgy and experience the joy of God's presence as tangibly as humanly possible alone on a country road. These prayer walks are no substitute for the real worship with my brothers and sisters in Christ each week at church. Still, this is a hidden jar of manna to sustain me with joy between Sundays. I feel fuller and happier after praying, even though and especially because there is no cell service here.

Prayer

Father in heaven,

I praise you for the gift of silence. It opens my heart and mind to hidden gifts in your creation. How I need this silence to slow down and focus on you.

I confess that I am often wooed by the allure of technology. Although technology is a gift as well, it easily takes me away from you. I need to lay it aside for set periods of my day to intentionally reconnect with you.

Thank you for the precious gift of worship, the calls in nature that invite me to glorify you with my reverence, praise, and songs. Thank you for opportunities to worship you alone and with others.

Guide me on this prayer journey, Lord. May it be a holy time of worship that sustains me throughout the week. May my walks in nature inspire new praise for the glory of your name.

I lift this prayer up in the name of Jesus.

Amen.

Reflection Questions

1. How can a daily break from technology cultivate a closer relationship between you and God?

2. Spend five minutes silently observing nature. What sounds did you hear? How did those sounds generate praise of our Creator?

3. How could the combined values of prayer walking and corporate worship enhance your spiritual growth?

CHAPTER TWO

MEMPHIS

Even a tree has more hope!
If it is cut down, it will sprout again
and grow new branches.
Though its roots have grown old in the earth
and its stump decays,
at the scent of water it will bud
and sprout again like a new seedling.

Job 14:7–9 NLT

My prayer-walking adventure would not exist without Memphis.
Our yellow Labrador retriever puppy needed lots of exercise. He
adored playing fetch several times per day, using his instincts and
his pouch-shaped mouth to retrieve his rubber toys. But I quickly
learned that three or four games of fetch cannot compare to the
joy he experiences on a walk—nor the hidden potential to wear
him out for a longer nap!

I looked at the walks as a win-win. He would get his exercise, and so would I. My plans were to take a brisk thirty-minute
walk each day at a steady 140-heartbeats-per-minute pace. Yet,
as with so many plans associated with this dog, his needs took

the forefront. That means we do a lot of starting and stopping on our walks. Memphis wants to stop and sniff more than he wants to walk. Walking is the means to get to his next sniffing station. Sometimes, he pokes his nose deep into the ditch, pushing it under the loose grass to get to the goodness underneath. He pauses at five or six predictable places along the fence line, beaten down with little paths that coyotes, raccoons, foxes, armadillos, and who knows what else have crawled under. Memphis inspects their leftover trails with the precision of an FBI detective, forming unseen files of data in his brain. He delights in absorbing as much scent as he can.

But I am impatient, especially when the winter wind is blowing from the north and cutting through my fleece pants. "Come on," I growl, yanking the leash. Yet Memphis is never ready to leave his sniffing post as soon as I am. Often, he plants his paws with force, insisting on staying even when I pull his collar down low enough to create dozens of furry wrinkles on his face. He sometimes stretches out his entire body on the ground, voluntarily choking himself, just to get a stronger whiff of his current open case. I have learned it's better to let him continue his sniff-capade as long as the scent requires. It's usually only a few moments longer than I want.

One study found that dogs that have more time for daily "nose-work" are more optimistic than dogs who were trained to heel.[1] Dogs need this time of olfactory stimulation to live up to their potential, like their ancestors who needed to develop this ability to forage for food. My Memphis isn't only enjoying his sniffing adventures; they are improving his quality of life.

These frequent stops on my prayer walks felt like rude interruptions at first, but I've learned to see them as gentle nudges from God to slow down and savor the pauses in my day. My prayer time is not at its best when I'm simply running down a list of requests as fast as I can. It's better as a meandering yet meaningful conversation, which includes pauses for meditating, silence, wonder, and delight.

I've learned that when Memphis needs to sniff, it's my cue to stop (even in mid-sentence), ponder, praise, rejoice, and surrender. It's the perfect time to thank God for all the joy that my furry boy has brought into my life; to mindfully delight in the many shades of white, yellow, gold, and reddish brown in Memphis's coat; to take notice of the sound of his intensive and repetitive sniffing, along with the rustling of the wind through the trees and the cries of the birds; to stop and marvel at one single moment in time when God is holding all things together in my body, on this country road, in this county, in this state, in this country, in this world, in this universe. I delight in how he pauses with me, delights in me, and shines his face upon me with a smile, all things I don't notice as often when I'm rushing forward, trying to get my steps in and my heart rate up.

Stopping and letting Memphis sniff has helped me be more mindful even when I'm not taking walks with him. For example, as I'm writing these book chapters in a three-week sprint, I'm pausing between each one. I step outside, breathe in the natural scents, feel the sun on my face, listen for the birds, run my fingers over Memphis's soft pelt, inhale the cinnamon-scented wax slowly burning, and savor a snack of apple slices and dark chocolate. These pauses are not frivolous; they are essential for nourishing my mind, body, and spirit so I can be the best writer, wife, mom, and friend I can be.

Without these pauses, I'm rushed and frazzled. My spirit dries up at a fast pace, and it feels like a dead stump. But if I pause a few times throughout the day to mindfully seek God and appreciate his ordinary yet lavish gifts, I recognize the scent of life-giving water, promised to us in John 4:13–14. It causes my hope, joy, and peace to bud and sprout again, flourishing with fresh leaves.

Prayer

Father in heaven,

I praise you for the beauty and refreshment in daily pauses. You surround me with loveliness if I choose to stop and take it in.

I confess that I am often running at a speed that doesn't allow me to appreciate all your blessings in my life. I choose hustle and hurry over mindfulness and meditation. But this leaves me sapped like a dead stump, which is not much use to you, me, or anyone else.

Thank you for showing me a new way today, Lord, a way that leads to fresh growth, a slow way that stops the hurry and takes in the full scent of life-giving water.

Remind me every time I feel stressed or impatient to pause and accept your grace and goodness. May the little pauses throughout my day refresh my spirit and draw me closer to you.

In Jesus's name,
Amen.

Reflection Questions

1. When are you most likely to feel stressed-out or impatient? How does this state limit your potential?

2. What are the best times of the day for you to take mindful pauses to appreciate simple blessings? Name four or five times of day you can take a two-minute pause, and decide the best way to be reminded to take them.

3. Where do you most need Jesus's life-giving water in your life? How can a daily pause help you find greater peace in that area?

NOTE

[1]Charlotte Duranton and Alexandra Horowitz, "Let Me Sniff! Nosework Induces Positive Judgment Bias in Pet Dogs," *Applied Animal Behaviour Science* 211 (2019): 61–66, ISSN 0168-1591, https://doi.org/10.1016/j.applanim.2018.12.009.

CHAPTER THREE

BRIDGE

I pour out my complaints before him
and tell him all my troubles.

Psalm 142:2 NLT

I mark the halfway point of my prayer walk at the bridge. It's a simple structure that marks a clear division and organizes my prayers. This bridge isn't fancy. It's a concrete structure with steel railings the county department paints yellow every other year or so. The bridge sits about fifteen feet above the waterline, where two little creeks converge. When the spring rains fill the creeks to their limits, the bridge is still high enough to allow vehicles to pass over.

This little bridge is located just before my turnaround point. Since it's halfway through my walk, I've decided to use it as a visual cue card to change my prayers. On days when I have a pressing concern, I don't always follow the liturgical format described in Chapter One. On those days, I pour out what's on my heart on the way to the bridge. On the way back home, I open my heart to receive and intercede.

The walk to the bridge is an ideal verbal and physical processing plant when my emotions are out of control. As soon as my shoes hit the driveway, I pour out the most stressful or frustrating thing before God. I verbally recap the events that caused my pain and ask God to help me find the truth gems hidden inside. Sometimes I enter a full-on rant, glad that only God and Memphis can hear what I'm saying. These rants are a relief because they relieve my internal pressure. Other times, I slowly unwind my ball of tangled thoughts, pausing several times to ask for God's wisdom and insight before I reach the bridge.

That walk to the bridge is a contained space for processing my junk. Since I have a mind that leans toward obsessing over details, I need a visual reminder to change prayer gears. The bridge is a hard stop. When I turn around on it, it's time to turn my prayers around too.

For a few minutes, I walk without speaking. In the quiet, I silently welcome God's presence and invite him alongside me. Many times, within a few moments of shutting my own mouth, the Holy Spirit speaks to my heart. With his whispers, he lavishes love on me, bringing favorite verses to mind. He sometimes corrects me and always comforts me. The insight he gives me once I quiet my spirit is a priceless treasure.

Then, I decide to use the rest of the walk home to intercede for the people involved in the problem about which I vented. God usually tucks prayer prompts for those people in the insights he just gave me. I pray along the lines of those insights, asking God to help me see them the way he sees them, to love them the way he loves them, even when they feel like my enemies. I ask him to help me remember I am not fighting against flesh and blood but against the dark powers of Satan's realm (Eph. 6:12). This truth about spiritual warfare strengthens my resolve to fight back with intercessory prayer.

After these processing prayer walks to the bridge and back, I always feel much better. A few times, I have needed to keep turning back to the bridge to continue processing the problem. Yet, without exception, I've returned home with greater peace in my heart, even if the problem did not get resolved while I was gone. The process of pouring out and then receiving and interceding helps me find peace that's tucked inside God's presence.

Many of us need visual reminders to pray. Many of us need time limits on our ruminating sessions. I'm thankful that God showed me how a bridge can indicate my need to change direction. It sets a time limit on my own words so I can make room for God's words to me. The bridge reminds me that prayer isn't only about pouring myself out to God. It's also about stilling myself in comfortable silence, waiting for his affirmation and direction. Prayer is also an assignment to lift others up to the Lord. If it weren't for the bridge, I might prattle on and on about my own junk, missing out on the blessing of the other prayer parts.

Now I look forward to reaching the bridge, not only because my venting session will be over and I'll feel relief, but because I'm excited to see what God will reveal if I listen. I'm eager to develop a more loving and compassionate attitude toward others through intercessory prayer, in which the Holy Spirit will guide me. The way back home from the bridge is an adventure in faith, which happens every time I first trust God with my complaints and troubles.

Prayer

Father in heaven,

I praise you for hearing my prayers, especially my troubles and complaints. I praise you for being big enough to handle them all and for being trustworthy to keep them totally safe.

I confess that I do not always switch gears in my prayers. Too often, I simply come asking for help. But I don't spend enough time praising you, waiting for your answers and praying for others with your guidance. I want to be more intentional, Lord.

Thank you for teaching me that I can choose reminders to redirect my prayers. Help me choose reminders along my prayer route to visually prompt me to listen to you and intercede for others.

When I am stressed, remind me that a prayer walk can be an ideal way to process my emotions in your presence. Meet me on those walks and teach me to hear your voice more clearly so that I can pray with greater confidence and compassion.

In Jesus's name,
Amen.

Reflection Questions

1. What do you normally do when you are stressed-out

   or frustrated? In the times you chose prayer to handle those times, did you experience greater peace? Why or why not?

2. What area of prayer would you like to practice with more intention—venting, listening, or interceding? How could your faith grow from being more intentional in this area?

3. What is a halfway point on your prayer journey? What visual marker can you use there to redirect your prayers?

CHAPTER FOUR

FERNS

*Let us hold tightly without wavering to the hope we affirm,
for God can be trusted to keep his promise.*

Hebrews 10:23 NLT

Even on the grayest late-winter days, I find signs of hope at the
base of a mighty oak tree. I can't see them from the warmth of my
home. I must brace myself against the cold to find them, and they
are always there.[1]

Because I battle a form of depression known as seasonal affective disorder, the last thing I want to do on a freezing February
morning is venture outdoors. I'd much rather stay bundled up with
my hot tea, Bible, blanket, and fuzzy socks in my toasty home. But
since Memphis nudges and paws at me while begging for his daily
walk, I sigh while I layer on my cold gear and clip on his leash.

Memphis and I travel a familiar path on these extra wintry
days. We stay in our own woods because the northern winds
on the gravel road are unbearable this time of year. We walk up
the gravel driveway, along the edge of the property, down to the
pond and across the levee, and into the woods on the northern
edge of the property. Memphis leads the way on a path cut by a

brush-hogger, making the woods much easier to navigate. We head straight down to the sandstone gully, stopping at the base of an enormous white oak tree. Its gnarled roots are covered in ferns—a welcome bright spot against the dry, dead leaves.

Since the root systems of ferns are shallow, they cling to the base of the tree for strength against chilly northern winds. Their lacy fronds look delicate, yet these native Missouri ferns are resilient when battered by rain, ice, and snow. They are a testament of strength in harsh elements.

Those tightly clinging ferns remind me of our key verse for this chapter: "Let us hold tightly without wavering to the hope we affirm, for God can be trusted to keep his promise" (Heb. 10:23 NLT). Here, the writer of Hebrews is referring to an eternal picture of hope: the most holy place in heaven, where we can boldly enter God's presence through prayer and receive a fresh infusion of hope as often as we need it. What a gift to enter God's presence this way no matter where we are—on a prayer walk or bundled inside. What a reason to celebrate even in the coldest of seasons!

But if you're like me, maybe hope has eluded you most of your life. Although I have always believed in God, I spent many years in survival mode against personal challenges like codependency, toxic relationship dynamics, boundary violations, and emotional abuse. I was fighting so hard to stay afloat mentally, emotionally, physically, and spiritually that I had no room to let hope in. When I dared to look toward the future, I saw cloudy gray, but little evergreen.

Several years ago, God began reorienting my vision. It started with daily Bible study in my One Year Bible. God met me over breakfast each day and taught me how much he loved me, no matter what lies I believed about myself. In new friendships with godly women within a small group at my church, he healed my wounds from broken relationships. During five years at the counselor's office, he helped me work through the hurts of my past, which took me out of survival mode. Then God showed me how to thrive in prayer, using hope in his promises as my anchor.

Just as the little ferns cling to the much bigger tree for strength, I have learned to cling to God when I need hope. He's always waiting for me on my prayer walks, delighting to wrap me in the warm embrace of his presence. He renews my vision with hope, which is green with abundant life in every situation, even on the coldest February day outside or the most frigid night in my heart.

Sometimes, I imagine God planted those ferns at the base of the white oak tree just for me. He uses them to remind me to fill my mind with the truth of his Word each day. God wants me to delight in the hope they represent, in the promise of spring even on the coldest days. He uses the ferns to direct my praise toward him, the One who uses anything he wants to draw us closer and give us new hope.

Prayer

Father in heaven,

I praise you for tucking signs of hope into my current season. You are faithful, kind, and loving to give me fresh hope each day. Open my eyes to see those signs planted just for me, Lord.

I confess that I often stay stuck in survival mode rather than turning my heart toward you with hope. It's easy for me to focus on my problems and get frozen in the past. But I want to see the green signs of hope while in your presence instead of focusing on the dry, dead parts of my life, which need revival from your living presence.

Thank you for your sunshine, which breaks through the clouds. It's strong enough to coax green to grow even on the coldest days, just as you are strong enough to give me hope in harsh storms.

Thank you for being so big that I can cling tight to you when I need your help. Thank you for the promise and hope of spring.

Help me hold tightly to the hope in your promises when I'm tempted to worry about the gray areas and cold seasons in my life. May your hope be evergreen in my heart and mind.

In Jesus's name,
Amen.

Reflection Questions

1. What feels gray, cold, or bleak in your life right now?

2. Which signs of green hope have you recently overlooked?

3. What steps will you to take to seek out God's green hope in your life every day in the next week?

NOTE

[1]A version of this chapter originally appeared as: Sarah Geringer, "Holding Tight to Hope," *Proverbs 31 Ministries*, Feb. 8, 2021, https://proverbs31.org/read/devotions/full-post/2021/02/08/holding-tight-to-hope.

CHAPTER FIVE

CHURCHES

Now I am departing from the world; they are
staying in this world, but I am coming to you.
Holy Father, you have given me your name;
now protect them by the power of your name
so that they will be united just as we are.

John 17:11 NLT

My mile-long walk begins at one church and ends at another. In our tiny town, never even incorporated, I am curious why the need for two churches arose.

On the surface, it seems that roughly one hundred people couldn't agree on particulars and thus decided to split. But perhaps there's a different story, one that God started writing generations ago for his glory.

The church closest to me used to own my property. They sold the fully wooded acreage to me so they could build a small fellowship hall. I sometimes walk around their cemetery and shaded church grounds because it feels peaceful there, and I can let Memphis off the leash for a while since he's familiar with the boundaries.

This church was first established in 1849, and its first constitution was drawn up in 1858. The present church building was constructed in 1896, and it still hosts weekly services.[1] I can hear its bell ringing every Sunday morning, right on schedule.

For a short period, my family and I were members of the other church at the end of my walk. That church was first built as a log building in 1866 and as a bigger brick building in 1868. Then, in 1900, that building was replaced by the one now standing.[2]

My great-grandparents were members of this church. I recall my great-grandmother telling me that the women sat on one side of the aisle and the men on the other. But she proudly said that my great-grandfather broke rank to sit with his family. Perhaps his action paved the way for the current free-for-all seating arrangement, and I am glad to know my crusader spirit stems from him.

Both websites state that details about church formation in our tiny town are shrouded in mystery, but local researchers know that people first gathered in house churches before any buildings were erected. Most of these people, including my ancestors, had fled Germany for religious freedom and opportunity, and they were eager to put their faith into practice.

Although no one knows exactly why this division occurred, I use the mystery to shape my prayers. These two beautiful buildings inspire me to pray for churches in my area, churches in my country, and churches around the world.

When the COVID-19 pandemic shut down all in-person church services, I prayed for members in tiny churches. Many of these elderly saints get out only for doctor's appointments, grocery store runs, and church services, so I know how important weekly worship is for their mental well-being. I knew it may be challenging for elderly people to convert to watching services online and challenging for pastors to convert to online ministry, so I kept praying for these two churches and for struggling small churches across the United States.

The sight of these churches at the beginning and middle of my walks reminds me never to take my faith for granted. They help me remember the sacrifices my ancestors made, only four generations ago, to board a ship en route to Missouri via the port of New Orleans to seek religious freedom. The buildings, seemingly strong and lasting, remind me how fragile our faith can be if we don't take deliberate steps to stand firm and pass it on to the next generation. I consider how proud my great-grandparents would be to see my children clinging to their faith, and it motivates me to keep praying for the next generations of believers.

As I ponder if the two churches were formed due to division, I pray for the divisions in the US church, divisions over non-negotiables in terms of orthodox belief, as well as negotiables that seem to divide us just as bitterly. I remember that right before his arrest, Jesus was praying for the unity of the church. He had believers for all time on his mind when he prayed that prayer—he was thinking of you and me. He wanted nothing more than for us to be united as he is united to the Father. "Oh," I sometimes cry out to God on my walks, "unite the churches in our nation, Lord! Because if we Christians can't show the world what unity looks like, who can?"

Finally, these two churches inspire my prayers for churches around the world. These include believers who can only practice their faith in house churches because they lack the freedom to worship, and they include my brothers and sisters in Christ who have no inkling of the clean, orderly, climate-controlled, Bible-filled churches I could walk into any Sunday. Yet their stories of exuberant worship in the direst conditions and in the face of brutal persecution drive me to my knees. I have never kneeled on the country road, but I have been humbled many times and have knelt in spirit by listening to testimonies about the persecuted church. What I hear most often is that they are desperate for our prayers, even more than for our money, so I continue to pray, and I also give.

I wonder if God led two groups in my area to establish two churches for positive reasons, to multiply the ministry opportunities, even if people couldn't agree on particulars. I'm glad that both churches continue to meet today, steadily plodding onward in this post-Christian culture. Their buildings hold more stories than I could possibly know, but I know God is at work in both.

Prayer

Father in heaven,

I praise you for the gift of church. You established it for my good, and you want me to be a part of it. What a joy and privilege!

I confess that I do not always see the value of the church. Sometimes I take it for granted. Often, I forget the sacrifices others made so I can worship in truth and freedom. Humble me, Lord. Remind me that you love the church, so I should too.

Thank you for the local churches in my area and for the churches across my nation and the world. Imperfect though they may be, I know you are working through them. Strengthen their members and grow their faith, Lord. Bless and guide their pastors and leaders as well.

Remind me to regularly pray for churches, Lord. Help me be an ambassador of unity, starting within my own church family. Teach me to value my faith heritage so I can stand firm and pass it on to others.

In Jesus's name,
Amen.

Reflection Questions

1. Who could you thank for passing their faith on to you?

2. Which churches in your area need your prayers? How might a commitment of praying for them each week help you pursue unity in your community?

3. What will you do to learn more about the persecuted church, and how can you pray more often for Christian brothers and sisters around the world? (A good place to start is persecution.com.)

NOTES

[1] "Saint James United Church of Christ Cemetery," Find a Grave, accessed October 20, 2021, https://www.findagrave.com/cemetery/2293771/saint-james -united-church-of-christ-cemetery.

[2] "Immanuel Lutheran Church History," Immanuel Evangelical Lutheran Church, accessed October 20, 2021, http://www.showme.net/churches /Immanuel/history.html.

CHAPTER SIX

GRASS

*The grass withers and the flowers fade, but
the word of our God stands forever.*

Isaiah 40:8 NLT

The winter landscape always looked bleak and boring to me before I started getting up close on my prayer walks. Now I see beauty even in the dead grasses of winter.

I took notice of the grass first by hearing the wind blow through it. The reedy sounds are silkier than the sound of wind blowing through tree branches. These subtly melodic songs helped me start appreciating what I once saw as just white, brown, or gray masses.

Grass covers every possible surface on the roadsides, pushing its way in between wildflowers and vines. The last uncut stems of Johnson grass are tall enough for me to brush with my hands. On warmer days, a resin from the seed heads lightly coats the tips of my fingers. Switchgrass covers the fields on either side of the gravel road. The seed heads form light brown clouds in places where the cows have not yet munched on them. The switchgrass mingles with clover, fescue, and timothy, patiently waiting for the warm sunrays of spring.

I see reddish-brown clumps of little bluestem on the levee of our pond and scattered here and there in the fields. Up close, I notice the fluffy white seeds, hairy tufts that are surprisingly tenacious in the punishing winds. I am also intrigued by the flattened seed clusters of river oats, which like to grow close to water. They make a nice addition to flower bouquets from the grocery store, a must-have item for my self-care routine in winter.

Finally, the wild rye seed heads are high on their tall stems, furry and spindled like the woolly worms that crawl on my porch. The color and striping patterns on the worms are said to predict the severity of winter weather. But the brown rye seed heads simply say it's winter as long as they are on the stems.[1]

These grassy textures delight me when the wildflowers I love so much aren't in bloom. They are a constant reminder of Jesus's parables, which often used nature to reveal profound truths. Jesus famously spoke about grass when telling us not to worry in the Sermon on the Mount. He said in Matthew 6:30 (NIV), "If that is how God clothes the grass of the field, which is here today and tomorrow is thrown into the fire, will he not much more clothe you—you of little faith?"

He had just said that the wildflowers of the field, tucked inside the grasses, are more magnificent than Solomon in all his splendor. Why? Because no one except God—not even the smartest scientist with the most sophisticated technology—can speak a wildflower or blade of grass into being. Humble though grass may be, it is still a reason to praise God for his magnificence as our Creator. It's also a reminder to refrain from worrying, because God is caring for us much more than he cares for all the grasses of all the fields, lawns, and roadsides in the world.

In the summer, the grass can become a burden because it grows faster than we can mow. The county department doesn't have enough equipment to mow all the Johnson grass to improve visibility on curvy roads, so sometimes a neighbor generously mows our roadsides with his tractor. I also need to constantly trim tall grass from around my mailbox, trees, and flowerbeds—my son takes care of mowing the rest. But in the winter, grass is no longer associated with a chore. Instead, it is a feast of visual and audible delights when I remember to appreciate it.

Whether in the fast-growing summer season or the sleepy winter season, the grasses on my prayer walk nudge me to remember the truth the Bible shares most often about grass: it is short-lived. Isaiah 40:6–7 compares people to grass, saying all of us will fall and all our lives are relatively short. Yet the hopeful truth is that the Word of God stands forever, and if I stand with God, I can live forever too.

The winter grasses cause me to ponder the question: What am I investing in today that will last forever? The answer is relationships, and for me, it is also writing and speaking. Those things are important and well worth my investment of time.

But I often underrate the time I spend with God in prayer. I think it can't matter as much to him as it does to me. I don't think I've ever doubted his love for me, but I have struggled to see that quality time with him matters on both sides of our relationship. Maybe this is due to my long-standing hang-up of needing and wanting quality time with others (it's my top love language, after all) but not receiving it in return. Yet the more often I meet with God in my prayer walks, the more I sense that he's delighting in the time with me even more than I delight in the time with him. I also sense that our times together somehow matter for eternity, and that's an area of wonder and mystery.

I love that in God's economy, nothing is wasted. Yes, people are like grass; our lives are short, and our seasons last for just a breath against the backdrop of all eternity. Yet because the Word of God stands forever, all the truth in it will last forever too. It points to his unchanging character, especially his everlasting love and unfailing kindness for us (Jer. 31:3). When I study the grass in winter, I praise God for his unchanging ways, and I take comfort in his constancy amidst all the changes in my life.

Prayer

Father God,

I praise you for your everlasting love and unfailing kindness to me. What a comfort it is to know that you never change your ways, even in all the changes I continually face.

I confess that I do not always remember that life is like grass—here today and gone tomorrow. I sometimes take things too seriously, and other times, I don't take things seriously enough. I fret and worry over things that don't last, and I forget that I, too, am like grass—short-lived compared to all eternity.

Thank you for the gift of many parables that teach us truths from nature. Your stories inspire me, Jesus. They help me ponder big truths in simple pictures. I thank you for bending down to help me understand your wisdom through Bible stories.

Help me remember that nothing is wasted in your economy, Lord. May I hold life loosely, treasuring it yet surrendering it to you at the same time. May the grasses in each season remind me of your timeless truths.

In Jesus's name,
Amen.

Reflection Questions

1. What feelings does the fact that God compares people to grass stir up in you?

2. Do you see grass as a chore? Do you see it as something more after reading this chapter?

3. How might you use the sight of grass as a prayer prompt?

NOTE

[1] I consulted this page for identification of common Missouri grasses: "Grasses," Missouri Department of Conservation, https://mdc.mo.gov /discover-nature/field-guide/grasses.

CHAPTER SEVEN

BURIED TREASURE

The kingdom of heaven is like treasure hidden in a field.
When a man found it, he hid it again, and then in his
joy went and sold all he had and bought that field.

Matthew 13:44 NIV

One Christmas morning when my boys were younger, they surprised me with a gift that came from our woods.

They had been doing their own excavating in preparation for building what they called a "hudget," a hut constructed of lumber scraps and fallen branches. In their expedition, they uncovered several buried treasures.

I'm a lover of antiques, so this box of goodies was one of my favorite presents. It's a collection of thirteen glass bottles that someone dumped in our woods several generations ago. Now the collection sits in the windowsills of our living room, and the diluted white winter light is perfect for studying these bottles.

They range in size from about two inches to twelve inches tall. Four have their original caps, rusted with age. All the rest are cap-free. Each of them is uniquely shaped, according to its contents. One is a honey jar, marked with the name of the manufacturer and a honeycomb pattern. Another clearly says "Borden's Malted Milk." Still another has numbers on either side to tick off ounces and milliliters (maybe for medicine?), with an iridescent sheen in certain light. A little one marked for chili powder bears an eagle logo. But the remainder keep me guessing what their contents may have been: perfume, lotion, ink, or something else? I haven't taken the time to research them online yet.

Another part I wonder about is why these bottles were buried at all. Like many people who survived the Great Depression, my great-grandparents saved everything, and I can't see them throwing bottles like these away. I imagine my great-grandfather would have stored nuts and bolts in these jars, and my great-grandmother would have reused them for her buttons. I find it unusual that someone buried a collection instead of reusing the bottles or hauling them to the junkyard.

But I'm not too surprised they buried them here in our woods, since we are its first inhabitants. No one would have known the bottles were buried here. Perhaps it was a group of children burying a treasure to discover later, and they forgot to dig it up. I did this as a child, and it delights me to think the children who may have played in our woods are now my grandparents' age.

This bottle collection is my own treasure and probably not worth much to anyone. They feel like treasure to me because they remind me that I'm linked to the past of this region. I'm permanently bound to this time in history and this place in the world, just like these bottles could be traced to specific manufacturers at specific times. They tell a story about the time they inhabited if I choose to uncover it. In the same way, I have a specific story and purpose right here, right now.

Only God knows what else is buried in my woods and the fields—arrowheads, broken clay dishes, and animal bones, to be sure. We have an unusual amount of sandstone in this area, which affects our water supply. Our well had to be drilled twice to push through all the clayey, sandy soil. Sometimes I wonder on my prayer walks if the great flood mentioned in Genesis 7 covered over the sandy beach that was once Missouri, thousands of years ago. I daydream about the layers of clay, rock, and silt built up over sand and the plethora of water deposits below; according to the well driller, there's enough water under our property to supply four houses for a lifetime. What was this place like when God first created it? It's fun to imagine.

The Bible tells us that the kingdom of God is like a treasure hidden in a field. It's highly valuable and just waiting to be discovered. When someone comes upon it, it's an enormous surprise and delight, like discovering a pot of gold in a field would be to us today.

Why does the man hide the treasure again once he discovers it? It's because he needs time to sell everything he owns to buy the field that houses the treasure. He auctions everything off and then purchases the field with overflowing joy. The field isn't the treasure—the kingdom of God is.

When we discover that the kingdom of God is in our reach, it's worth everything we can afford to get it: heart, soul, mind, and strength (Mark 12:30 NIV). With this large investment of ourselves, we get pure joy thrown in. Only some of us will be called to sell everything we have to follow Jesus (see Mark 10:17–31), but all of us are called to give ourselves up as living sacrifices and whole-heartedly follow God rather than the world (Rom. 12:1–2).

As one who has given up her heart, soul, mind, and strength for the Lord, I can tell you it's worth every single sacrifice I've made. The joy he gives me despite many trials is like glowing jewels hidden in the woods and fields around me. I dig them back up during my prayer walks, recounting God's faithfulness to me. I trust he will help me uncover more buried treasures of faith as I continue to meet with him in prayer.

Prayer

Father God,

I praise you for including me in your kingdom. What a joy it is to serve you as my king! What a privilege it is to be your beloved child, adopted into your forever family.

I confess that I do not always look for the signs of your kingdom hidden in my life. I forget to praise you for your faithfulness to me. I do not follow you with all my heart, mind, soul, and strength. But I recommit myself to you today.

Thank you for promising to give me great joy if I give up everything for you, Jesus. Thank you that in return for my heart, soul, mind, and strength, I get eternal life and all the riches of your heavenly inheritance, plus a vibrant relationship with the Lord of lords.

Remind me to offer myself up as a living sacrifice every day, Father. May I not seek the glitz and glamour of the world, but may I go on daily expeditions for the hidden treasures in prayer.

In Jesus's name,
Amen.

Reflection Questions

1. What treasures did you bury or dig up as a child?

2. What purpose does God have for you in this specific time and place?

3. Which treasures of God's kingdom would you like to discover in prayer?

CHAPTER EIGHT

COYOTE

Today I have given you the choice between life and death,
between blessings and curses. Now I call on heaven and
earth to witness the choice you make. Oh, that you would
choose life, so that you and your descendants might live!

Deuteronomy 30:19 NLT

On cold, clear winter nights, I can hear the coyotes howling in groups. They don't scare me; in fact, I welcome this sound of life in the dead of winter.

One winter day, as I walked the path with Memphis, I noticed a strange shape in the creek. Upon closer inspection, I noticed it was a dead coyote lying just beneath the surface of the water. I couldn't tell if someone dumped it there or if it had fallen to disaster.

The sight of this coyote brought hot tears to my eyes, which quickly turned cold in the winter air as they ran down my cheeks. My highly sensitive and empathic heart was overloaded not only by the sight of this poor animal but by a long season of collective and personal grief.

I saw the coyote on a winter morning nearly a year and a half after the pandemic began. There was so much focus on death and the fear of death for so long, I wondered if the news stories would ever end. Now, as I write this in the fall of 2021, the stories of death keep unfolding by the day.

I remembered the fear that gripped me when I was told to go to the emergency room for a virus test, since my symptoms included shortness of breath. That November morning, I looked around my home in a panic. Would I be admitted? Was I sicker than I felt? Panic coursed through me as I drove to the hospital, and I fought back by meditating on Isaiah 26:3 over and over and reading *Trusting God* by Jerry Bridges in the waiting room. Four hours later, I was released yet shaken. I had received a sharp reminder that my life itself is but a breath (Job 7:7), and if God would withdraw from me, I would turn right back into the dust from which I am formed (Job 34:14–15).

Grief had gripped me in late 2020 in the near-death of a loved one, estrangement in several relationships, and private sorrow too personal to share. This was after months of grieving the loss of daily life as we knew it in many unforeseen ways. The sight of the coyote pushed all this grief to the front for a moment, and I poured out my heartache to God on the country road, tears streaming and nose running.

Surprisingly, the annoyance of my nose running without an available tissue reminded me that I was alive, that my body still reacted to the elements and acted in gracious response to my grief by keeping my breathing passages lubricated. I pulled back my coat and wiped my nose with my sleeve, grinning through my tears as I thanked God for the gross yet helpful reminder.

Too often, my melancholy nature focuses on the negative. This is especially true in late winter when I've battled seasonal affective disorder for several months in a row. I just want the persistent gray clouds to break up, the sun to shine clearly on one single day. Yet the sun often stays hidden in my part of the country this time of year. I must choose to see life when the gray tries to hide it from me.

When I turned away from the coyote, I thanked God for caring for all the wild animals who belong to him, including the ones hidden from my eyes but living and breathing right then in the woods, known fully by the Lord. I thanked him for the life hidden underground—the roots of the grasses and flowers, the sap flowing through the trees, the bud cells buried inside branches, the many animals and insects burrowed beneath the earth, hearts slowed to conserve energy yet still very much alive.

Then I focused on my Memphis. I saw the plumes of hot air flowing from his open mouth. As the sun peeked through the clouds, it caught the glint of the pure golden hairs on his back, dazzling with glitter. I listened to his steady panting and watched his tail wag. Life, right in front of me. What a gift worth celebrating.

Before the Hebrews crossed into the promised land, Moses exhorted them to choose well. He told them to choose between life and death, between blessings and curses. He knew that their sinful nature would always lead them to choose death and curses. But in Deuteronomy 30:20, he stated that the choice for life required love, obedience, and commitment to God. Then the promises of the covenant relationship would hold true in their lives.

This is the choice I still need to make every time I take a prayer walk. I need to choose to see the life that exists in loving God, obeying him, and staying committed to him no matter what. When I compared that life to how I feel when I go my own way, the best choice is clear. I experience greater peace, joy, and hope when I practice these things, and I sense the Spirit's life in me as I pursue them.

Although the coyote was washed away by spring rains long ago, I still reflect on the wisdom I gained by seeing it. I need to remember that pondering death for a prescribed time is wise according to the Bible (Eccles. 7:4). But I also need to remember that God wants me to choose life over death (Eccles. 8:15) and to keep praying as long as I have breath (Ps. 116:2).

Prayer

Father in heaven,

I praise you for the gift of life. Without your breath in me, I would be nothing. You both give and sustain my life, and I am grateful to you.

I confess that I do not always focus on life. Instead, I focus too much on death and sorrow. Fear keeps me captive in negativity. I also sometimes take life for granted. Forgive me, Lord.

Thank you for the signs of life all around me if I choose to see them. Thank you for sustaining life even in the hidden places because you are the owner of all things. If you lovingly care for the wild animals, surely you are caring even more for me, since I am made in your image.

Help me choose life in all my attitudes today. I want my love, obedience, and commitment to you to grow. May my faithful prayers connect me to the spirit of life you place in me.

In Jesus's name,
Amen.

Reflection Questions

1. What signs of death did you see during the pandemic? How did these signs affect your faith?

2. In which areas of your life do you need to choose life over death?

3. In what practical ways will you show love to God, obey him, and commit yourself to him this week?

CHAPTER NINE

CEDARS

Accept my prayer as incense offered to you, and
my upraised hands as an evening offering.

Psalm 141:2 NLT

If there is any tree I associate with southeast Missouri, it's the eastern red cedar. It's our most common evergreen tree, and it grows in many places along my prayer walk.

To farmers, this tree can be a nuisance since it shoots up quickly right in the middle of valuable cattle pastures. Birds love its sweet, waxy blue berries and deposit them everywhere, so this tree grows freely. One of the farmer's winter chores is digging up the baby cedar trees from the fields before they grow too tall. This tree is too prickly to grab bare-handed—you need leather gloves to work with it—and its taproot grows deep. Removing these trees can be a real chore on a winter afternoon. I must dig baby cedars out of my woods too.

But I love these cedars anyway. Their scent is Christmas to me, because my great-grandparents always had this variety as their holiday tree, and a farmer always donated a huge cedar tree to my childhood church for its Christmas programs. But since the branches are weak, they can handle only the lightest ornaments.

Ornaments fashioned from Styrofoam, straw, paper or feathers, and the prerequisite silver tinsel are ideal for these trees. The tangy, aromatic fragrance of the trees would fill my great-grandparents' home and the entire church with a warm ambiance.

Many of the trees on my walk have been trimmed by the county department so they don't interfere with the power lines. Their shapes are funny and distorted, far less beautiful than their natural conical shape. Yet the birds love taking shelter in the dense evergreen tinged with bronze. On my winter walks, I see bright red male cardinals flitting in and out of the branches, chasing the taupe-colored ladies and snacking on the blue fruits.

Technically, the eastern red cedar that grows here is not a true cedar. The eastern red cedar belongs to the *Juniperus* family, while true *Cedrus* trees grow in Europe and Asia.[1] However, I associate my local cedar tree with worship, which is what the Bible most often associates with cedar trees.

Cedar sticks were used in the purification rites that priests performed to symbolize the removal of sins (see Lev. 14). Cedar was also prime construction material for Solomon's Temple. Solomon commissioned a supply of cedars from King Hiram of Tyre, who sent them from the Lebanese forests (see 1 Kings 5). This wood formed the walls and the covering for everything in the temple, which was overlaid in gold (1 Kings 6:18, 22, 36).

In my imagination, I have long thought of cedar trees lined up along the fence rows as priests in a procession line. They are celebrating in high church form, like I have witnessed in local Catholic services. Their robes are gilded with bronze details, and they march in quiet and reverent confidence toward the altar, where the priest who carries the ball of smoking incense will offer prayers on behalf of the people.

Whether I am walking on my prayer walk on the country road or zipping along I-55 north toward St. Louis, I take notice of the procession lines of eastern red cedars. I consider their scent in the church sanctuary from Christmases when I was young, and I imagine God savoring their sharp aroma like a pleasing incense. I see the light catch on the bronze tips of their branches in late February, exposing a reddish-brown undertone, and it reminds me of the sacrifice of the lamb for all time, the holy One we worship.

I know that God longs for me to offer up my prayers to him. They are a sweet-smelling incense that pleases him as the cedar scent pleases me. I'm relieved I don't have to perform the purification rites like an ancient Israelite. Nor do I need to don the fancy robes I would need for a high church service. I can simply put on my athletic shoes, cold-weather leggings, winter coat, scarf, gloves, and hat and be just as proper in God's eyes. He simply wants me out there on the road, even in the late February cold, singing and shouting my praises to him. I'm amazed at how he transforms the hot breath from underneath my scarf into aromatic incense when I pray.

On certain days, when the winter sun is bright and gets the resins flowing in the cedar trees, I catch a whiff of that pleasing aroma again. It ties me to beloved Christmas memories, and it also reminds me how precious my prayers are to my Lord, how delighted he is when I worship him in procession with the cedars, because the trees of the field are clapping in celebration of his glory, singing about his joy and peace (Isa. 55:12).

Prayer

Father God,

I praise you for accepting my worship as if it is a sweet incense to you. I'm grateful that I can come as I am to you, and you love all my prayers even if they aren't fancy.

I confess that I don't always prioritize worship. I doubt that my prayers mean much to you, and I forget to worship you with songs from a glad heart. Move me to praise you every time I pray.

Thank you for treasuring my prayers and valuing my worship. You do not need my attention, but you long for it all the same. What a joy and privilege it is to offer you my humble prayers and praise, O King of kings.

Help me prioritize private worship of you, Lord. May the songs of my heart and the incense of my prayers be a source of joy for both you and me. May the times I spend praising your character draw me closer to you in deep appreciation.

In Jesus's name,
Amen.

Reflection Questions

1. How do you think God receives your prayers?

2. Do you feel like you need to dress yourself up before you begin prayer or worship? Why or why not?

3. How could private worship, in addition to corporate worship, increase your closeness with God?

NOTE

1 "Eastern Red Cedar," Missouri Department of Conservation, accessed October 22, 2021, https://mdc.mo.gov/discover-nature/field-guide/eastern-red-cedar.

SPRING

CHAPTER TEN

BIRDSONG

Look, the winter is past,
and the rains are over and gone.
The flowers are springing up,
the season of singing birds has come,
and the cooing of turtledoves fills the air.

Song of Solomon 2:11–12 NLT

One of the surest signs that spring has finally arrived are the bird-songs that greet me with the dawn. They inspire me to explore my prayer walk path with fresh curiosity.

I have long been a bird lover. During my weekly trips to the regional library, I enjoyed visiting the finches in their cage near the library card drawers. Their quiet twittering was lovely background noise while I searched for new reads.

I also loved watching birds at my father's house, not too far from where I now live. He had several feeders set up in his yard that faced the woods. In the summer, dozens of gold and red finches would fly out of the woods and wait impatiently on the power line, jockeying for their time to gorge on black nyjer seeds. Their bright yellow coats were like rays of sunshine in my tough high school years, calming me for a moment with their natural beauty.

One of my favorite parts of living in the woods is dwelling among many varieties of wild birds. I know them mostly from their visits to my feeders, not by their individual songs—but I am learning. All winter long, the Canadian juncos join the local chickadees, cardinals, Carolina wrens, white-breasted nuthatches, tufted titmice, blue jays, robins, and several types of woodpeckers for a sunflower seed feast. They still appreciate the seed in spring when they busy themselves with nest building, and I hope the extra seed will help them have more eggs in each nest.

Setting out for a walk in early spring, I still need my jackets and cold gear in the morning. But the reward for my time in layering is the cheery birdsong in my woods and in the thickets and tree stands along the gravel road. Their songs, so innocent and happy, remind me to delight in the new life that is sprouting all around me.

Spring always wrestles with winter to gain the upper hand. Cold, windy mornings vie for power against the warmer, sunny afternoons. Yet the birdsong is consistent. Right at dawn, the timing of which aligns with the morning bus pickup, the birdsong volume increases moment by moment. They join in chorus with local roosters to welcome the sun's rays no matter the March morning temperatures.

The songs of the birds remind me to sing my own in heartfelt praise to God. Sometimes, I take my old iPhone 3 on my walks, because it has music stored in its own library (no streaming necessary). The Christian praise songs I downloaded on iTunes years ago are still perfect for my personal praise times. The birds are the backup singers, and I take the lead while covering these favorites from a few years back. I join in those familiar melodies to convert my prayers to musical form.

Prayers set to music are a sweet melody to the Lord. They lift my heart on days when gray winter gets the upper hand, not just outside but in my mood as well. Musical prayers take the load off when I don't feel as if I have fresh words to share or when I feel stuck on a certain issue. They remove the blockage and inspire new directions for praise, worship, thanksgiving, and requests.

Listening to the same songs in new situations reminds me of God's faithfulness. The songs I chose in past seasons put me back in times when I cried out to God for help in past situations. Now I can see those situations through the lens of hindsight, which always leads me to praise God for his past faithfulness. Using hindsight now renews my hope that if God heard and answered my prayers then, he is already preparing answers for my prayers now. The songs are a gateway to accessing that hope.

The birdsongs themselves are another reminder of God's faithfulness. Year after year, the birds faithfully trumpet their praise to God. They were created to sing, and in this way, they glorify their Creator. I, too, am part of God's creation, and one of my purposes is to sing his praise day after day, year after year. The birds' cheerful songs, no matter the temperature, remind me that I can choose to praise him no matter my circumstances.

My prayer walks help me see birds that do not visit my feeders. Missouri bluebirds, who prefer worms and mosquitoes to birdseed, flit out of cover as I draw near the streams they love. I also see blue flashes from indigo buntings, who love picking the last remaining seeds from the slowly greening fields. Mourning doves coo in the branches of the oak trees, and their repetitive cries remind me to meditate over and over on God's truths.

My prayer walks would not be the same without the birds. Their lovely chorus, especially bright in spring, signals the change of seasons and prompts new praises from my heart.

Prayer

Father God,

I praise you for the beauty of birds. You created them for your glory, and we can see glimpses of your glory through their songs. I thank you for the loveliness of birdsong, which is a sign of the arrival of spring.

I confess that I do not always praise you with a cheerful heart. Sometimes I go through the motions of faith, and I get stuck in the doldrums of winter. But I want a fresh start, and I want to greet new seasons with joy, just as the birds do.

Thank you for inspiring me to praise you through songs. Whether I sing them to you on my prayer walks or just listen along to recordings or the birds themselves, may my heart lift in joyful worship and gratitude for your faithfulness.

Remind me that the rising of the sun on a new day is always a reason to praise you. Help my heart be tuned to your reminders to praise you, day after day and season after season, just as the birds faithfully praise you with their songs.

In Jesus's name,
Amen.

Reflection Questions

1. When is the best time for you to take notice of birds?

2. Do you tend to greet the morning with praise or grumbling? How could listening for birdsong in the morning inspire you?

3. Which recorded songs put you in a worship mode, and which ones remind you of God's faithfulness to you in past seasons?

CHAPTER ELEVEN

THRONG

Hope deferred makes the heart sick, but
a dream fulfilled is a tree of life.

Proverbs 13:12 NLT

In April 2020, I was waiting for life to return to normal, when I could go to town without thinking, just for fun; when I could go to church services and Stephen Ministry training without worrying about close contact; when my sixteen-year-old son with a March birthday could finally take his driver's license test; and when all three of our children could return to school.[1]

One morning that April, Memphis could hardly wait to go on a walk. His whole body wagged when I said that magic word. Since the morning was cool, I donned my winter coat and grabbed my phone before clipping the leash on his collar.

Signs of spring welcomed us right away, and I took delight in snapping photos. Birds were chirping. Bright green moss was spreading. Spring beauty flowers nodded their heads in the slight breeze. Grape hyacinths greeted the day. The mayapples twirled their parasols. The white blooms on the serviceberry tree smiled back at me. The still-closed redbud blossoms whispered, *Come back tomorrow and see us open up.*

Memphis and I walked down the hill, where the paved county road turns into gravel. There, he stuck his snout into something interesting at the base of a mustard plant. These knee-high plants always bloom bright yellow at the beginning of spring. A cole crop, they aren't bothered by the swings between cold and warm temps this time of year.

As my pup sniffed the plant base, the yellow petals fell on his face and ears. He delighted in a scent I couldn't detect. We turned onto the gravel county road where we most enjoy our walk. It's as if we have that quiet road all to ourselves on spring mornings.

Heading northward, mustard plants filled the roadsides. They seemed held back only by the gravel on the left and the fence on the right. Their yellow blossoms, too hard to miss, declared joy in unison.

We continued walking down the road, through the woods and beside the cow pasture to the bridge. By the water, an even greater throng of mustard plants sang their hallelujah chorus to our Creator.

Many of us had sick hearts that spring because our hope had been deferred. Parties were postponed. Sports seasons were stopped. Graduations were up in the air. Weddings were moved months ahead. Vacations were canceled.

We all had something to grieve in that season, including losses of freedom, health, convenience, or comfort. Adjusting to the new normal, overnight, was exhausting. We will never forget that spring of struggle.

When our hearts feel sick, it is tempting to get off track with the wrong things, such as emotional things like bitterness, self-pity, and grudges; relational things like lashing out, withdrawing, and complaining; and pleasurable things like too much food, wine, television, or social media.

If we learn nothing else from that challenging spring, may it be that we must place our hope in our Creator alone.

Spring is God's idea. I don't think it's any coincidence that the pandemic first occurred in the northern hemisphere when hope begins blooming outside our doors.

God has infused the Christian life with so much hope that it sticks to one's face, one's hands, and one's heart, just as the mustard flower blossoms couldn't help but stick to Memphis's fur. This hope is rooted in Isaiah 53:5–6, which tells us Jesus suffered for our sake so we could be healed and whole. We can reach out and touch this hope, turn it over, and study its brightness through meditation and prayer.

Isaiah wrote that passage hundreds of years before the Messiah was born. He hoped in a Messiah to come. We now stand on the other side of that hope as Easter people. We are looking forward to the hope in Jesus's return, when he will take us where the tree of life will heal the nations.

Our hearts can become sick with hope in the wrong things. If we place our ultimate hope in people, places, events, institutions, and even our dreams, we will surely lose hope, because the whole world as we know it is passing away.

But if we place our ultimate hope in God alone, he will be a tree of life for us.

Jesus said if we have faith as small as a mustard seed, nothing is impossible for us. Maybe a mustard plant was brushing his knee when he spoke those words. Perhaps later, he held a seed from that plant in his hands when he compared a mustard seed to the kingdom of God. A seed you plant in your heart can become a tree of life, a tree with yellow blossoms of hope that will prosper in every season, no matter the changes life brings.

Prayer

Heavenly Father,

I praise you for tucking hope into every corner of my life, in every season.

I confess that I often focus on the muddy road, rocky path, cold winds, or gray clouds instead of opening my eyes to the yellow blossoms of hope that bloom bright every day.

Thank you for being my tree of life, which does not wither in any season.

Help me look for signs of hope so my heart will be whole, not sick. May I put my trust in you alone when I feel discouraged so I can sing "hallelujah" to you every day.

In Jesus's name,
Amen.

Reflection Questions

1. What losses hit you hardest at the beginning of the pandemic?

2. In which areas has your heart grown sick due to deferred hope?

3. Which yellow blossoms of hope have you seen in the past week?

NOTE

[1] A version of this chapter originally appeared on Sarah Geringer, "Waiting When Hope is Deferred," *Sarah Geringer*, April 15, 2020, https://www .sarahgeringer.com/waiting-hope-deferred/.

CHAPTER TWELVE

SPRING RAINS

And yet, O Lord, you are our Father.
We are the clay, and you are the potter.
We all are formed by your hand.

Isaiah 64:8 NLT

The spring rains, often bringing inches of water at a time, sometimes reshape the gravel road. The water pours down the hilly pasture, overflowing the ditches and carving deep ruts on the eastern side. The county department then brings out heavy equipment to move the heavy clay back into place and cover it with new gravel.

When Memphis and I discover this situation on our morning walks, we reroute our path. Since I know how much strength it takes to shovel the heavy clay soil in my garden, I marvel at how much water must flow to wash out half a country road. The power of the water amazes me.

I have grumbled against this clay, which stunts the growth of many plants. I have spent hundreds of dollars amending the soil in my gardens, adding peat moss, compost, and vermiculite to break up the clods of clay. However unhelpful this clayey soil is for gardening, it is perfect for making pots.

When I was a student at the local university, I spent a semester as a museum intern. I got to select pieces to display in the gallery and hallways. In my findings, I delighted in choosing from a collection of prehistoric Native American artifacts, created from the clay right here in southeast Missouri.

The pots were swirled with several colors of clay: white, tan, red, brown, and black. Hands once shaped them into vases, plates, cups, and serving dishes. I admired these pieces for both their practicality and beauty.

To pursue my art degree, I was required to take several sculpture classes. The clay always needed moisture to be workable. If it dried out between sessions, we had to moisten it again so it would become soft. The heat from our hands also helped the clay remain pliable.

As I walk the gravel road, I wonder if wives and mothers like me once took the clay from this very region in their hands, carefully picking out the rocks and debris. I imagine them mixing this clay with water collected from spring rains to shape it into the dishes that would hold their suppers, warming it in their supple grasp. They may have baked their creations in fires right in these fields, cooling them on collected branches of trees long gone, yet living on in the ancestry of seeds I now see as tall trees in front of me.

The power of the spring rains to shape the clay of the road reminds me of the power God's hands hold to shape my life. It is not my right to argue with him about the purposes for which he created me, no more than a clay pot has the right to criticize its maker (Isa. 29:16). Instead, I want to yield to the warmth and softness of his hands as he shapes me. He often uses the rains of sadness and sorrow to soften the soil of my heart, to make it more useful for his plans. He picks out the rocks and removes the thorns, amending the clay so it is more valuable and useful (Luke 8:4–15).

I must admit, it often does not feel good when God is stretching and shaping me. Yes, his hands are both tender and strong. But I don't always want to submit to this hard kneading, even when it's for my good. I'd rather have the sunny days with no spring rains, although the water softens the clay of my heart. I resist God's removal of rocks and thorns, often settling for the second-best versions of the world's offerings for my needs and desires.

But when I finally lay still and let God shape me how he wants, God gives me hope that I can become a beautiful vessel set apart for his special use rather than a common one (Rom. 9:21). With his shaping, I can become a fragile clay jar that carries the light of the Lord, not boasting of anything in myself, but projecting his glory (2 Cor. 4:7). I always feel better in the end when I admit that I am the humble clay, and he is the master potter. As I look back on my life during my prayer walks, I can trace God's shaping in my life, which has always been for my good and for his glory.

Prayer

Father God,

I praise you as my potter, who shapes me as your clay. It's good to remember that you are in control of all things in my life and that I need to submit to you in everything.

I confess that I often resist your shaping. I don't like the rains that soften me. I don't want you to remove the rocks and thorns because I think they bring me comfort you'd be much better at providing. Forgive me for criticizing the purposes for which you have created me.

Thank you for shaping my life with your warm, strong, tender hands. Thank you that a little bit of spring rain can make the clay of my heart pliable once again. Thank you for masterfully building me up for your glory.

Help me hold still under your loving touch. May I accept the rains in my life as necessary for my spiritual growth. May I submit to whatever purpose you have for me so I can be used to carry your light to others.

In Jesus's name,
Amen.

Reflection Questions

1. What clay objects do you use on a regular basis?

2. Do you welcome the rains in your life, or do you resist them? Why?

3. If you submitted to God's shaping in a certain area rather than criticizing it or fighting it, what good may come from your surrender?

CHAPTER THIRTEEN

LOCKDOWN

And you who are left in Judah,
who have escaped the ravages of the siege,
will put roots down in your own soil
and grow up and flourish.
For a remnant of my people will spread out from Jerusalem,
a group of survivors from Mount Zion.
The passionate commitment of the LORD of Heaven's Armies
will make this happen!

Isaiah 37:31–32 NLT

As an avid gardener, I am a keen observer of changes from year to year in my flowerbeds and woods. I can honestly say that in all the years of living on our property, no more beautiful spring has existed than the spring of 2020.

I truly believe God gave us a special dispensation of beauty that spring to counterbalance all the grief and loss we were experiencing. After years of observing this property, I had no doubt God was displaying his glory in a new way during a season that seemed dark, and he chose to do that through nature.

It started with my forsythia bush at the top of the driveway. It was the first year it bloomed, and the yellow blooms brightened my mood right when the confusing news started rolling in.

Would everything really be canceled? I doubted this as I continued with my plans to speak at a local women's luncheon on Saturday, March 15. As I got ready that morning, I clearly sensed the Lord speaking to me with an undertone of warning: "Enjoy this day, Sarah." I thought he was speaking to my hard-driven, perfectionist nature that is prone to push forward without stopping to celebrate. But in hindsight, I now know he was encouraging me to soak up the sweetness of that last live speaking event I would have in many months.

Yet, as I pulled into my driveway on the way home from that blessed event, the yellow forsythia cheerily greeted me. It was the first sign of the abundant beauty that would unfold that spring as a special grace to all of us.

My pink and magenta peonies have never bloomed so beautifully, nor have they been scented with such sweet perfume. Irises that had laid dormant opened back up with stately white, purple, and burgundy blooms. My azalea bushes burst with hot pink glory. My serviceberry tree had so many white blossoms that spring, it yielded enough blueberry-like fruits that I used them for the first time in the kitchen, baking them into a delicious lemon pound cake.

With abundant rains in the spring of 2020, the greening trees never looked so fresh. Spring beauty, a delicate white flower, popped up everywhere in our woods. The lawn and roadsides bloomed with crowds of purple and yellow violets, seas of white and pink clover, and clumps of smiling buttercups. I was even glad to see the extra profusion of sunny dandelion blooms, since their joyful faces seemed to defy the spirit of death permeating the news. Many tiny flowers sparked joy all around me, too abundant to ignore.

Although I felt locked down on this property from mid-March through the rest of the spring season, God's lavish love for me was undeniable, showcased in nature each day. On every prayer walk, my eyes feasted on the abundant flowers—everything I've listed before, plus the lavender wild sweet William, bluish-purple periwinkle, daffodils, grape hyacinths, and tiny violas in their finest spring parade ever.

During those long months that felt like a siege, with our supplies and socialization cut off, it was easy for us to grumble and complain. It was easy to choose fear over faith and doubt over deliverance. Yet God was planting something new in those of us who chose to stay faithful, just as he preserved his remnant in Judah during the Babylonian siege.

There is still time for us today to put roots of faith down into our own soil that can grow up and flourish for the greater good. The Lord of Heaven's Armies is still on our side, especially on prayer walks. He fills the hills and valleys all around us with his angel armies, who will come alongside us in our spiritual battles. We can be reminded of God's presence and glory as we seek out the beauty all around us, too profuse to be missed, often spotted in wildflowers.

As I reflect on the abundance of spring's glory in 2020, I am inspired to seek out signs of life in the sieges I feel like I'm under today. I take those matters to God on my prayer walks now, reflecting on his goodness to me in that tough season. If he displayed his love and glory in such lavish ways then, surely he has it on display for me somewhere now. I only need to gain awareness of it, and I pray that God will open the eyes of my heart to it now, when I'm no longer in the same lockdown as before.

Prayer

Father God,

I praise you for releasing me from the lockdowns of the past, the sieges that have battered my heart. I praise you for the promise of new life.

I confess that I grumble and complain rather than praising and trusting. I choose fear and doubt over a greater commitment to you. I take my eyes off the glory you display all around me, the signs of hope you tuck in nature every day. Forgive me for my negativity that blocks the beauty of your presence.

Thank you for the promise of new life even after siege-like seasons. Thank you for surrounding me with angel armies of protection in the spiritual places. Thank you for equipping me to fight in my spiritual battles so I can overcome for your glory.

May the roots of your Word push deep into my heart and grow up and flourish for your glory. May your passionate commitment to me be a constant source of hope.

In Jesus's name,
Amen.

Reflection Questions

1. What did you notice about nature in the spring of 2020?

2. What seasons of your life have felt like lockdowns or sieges?

3. How can the lessons you learned in the spring of 2020 strengthen your faith now?

CHAPTER FOURTEEN

DAISIES

The Sovereign LORD *will show his justice to the
nations of the world. Everyone will praise him!
His righteousness will be like a garden in early
spring, with plants springing up everywhere.*

Isaiah 61:11 NLT

The daisies in May bloom on the roadsides. I know the exact
places where they bloom—at the bottom of the hill in the shade,
and right in front of the gate on the gravel road. They are scattered
in the fields as well, little painter's dabs of white against new green.

I admire the daisies' ability to withstand the May breezes.
Although the flower heads look top-heavy on the stems, they easily
sway with either a chilly blast from the north or a warm wind from
the southwest. Their yellow faces always point upward toward the
sun, with white petals streaming outward in praise.

In all my walks when I have spied these flowers, I have never
picked even one. But when I was a child, I played the common he-
loves-me, he-loves-me-not game with daisy petals. Now, these
flowers represent much more than a lonely girl's question to me.

These daisies on my prayer walk are living symbols of Bible promises to come. They seem to hold the peaceful promises of Isaiah 40–61 inside their little forms. After thirty-nine chapters warning about destruction and judgment, God's words spoken through Isaiah switch to hope and peace. They are comforting and encouraging, with promises for both then and for the future that still awaits.

After long, hard seasons in my life, the daisies have been a welcome testimony of hope. They are white and fresh, reminding me that Jesus is making all things new (Rev. 21:5) in his kingdom of righteousness. When the winters of my struggles have seemed too harsh, and spring never seemed as if it would arrive, the real daisies on my prayer walks helped me rejoice that God's promises are true.

Over and over in the book of Isaiah, God promises to bring life where there once was death: crocuses in the wastelands (Isa. 35:1), streams in the wilderness (Isa. 35:6), new growth where desert animals once lived (Isa. 35:7). He promises that his people will be like well-watered gardens, a picture of royalty in ancient times, because only kings could afford gardens with bountiful supplies of water (Isa. 58:11).

As believers, we are part of this promised kingdom Isaiah wrote about eight hundred years before Jesus was born. Someday, his justice will reign among all the nations of the world. Someday, every tongue will declare Jesus as Lord (Phil. 2:11). And God's righteousness, now planted as wheat among weeds (Matt. 13:24–30), will bloom everywhere. Its beauty will no longer be obscured by sin but will be on full display like May daisies, with their peaceful faces blowing in the breeze, inviting you to ponder God's promises.

For now, I must settle for daisies blooming in just a few places along my prayer walk. Their blooms last perhaps three weeks and then fade once the summer heat arrives. Sometimes I bend to touch their faces, to finger their nubby centers. Feeling them in my hands, I pause to absorb God's peace in a quiet moment that only he sees.

The hope of heaven often falls to the side in my daily walk of faith. It sits in the margins, crowded out by more immediate prayer concerns like bills that need to be paid, relationships that need repair, friends who are dealing with sickness or sorrows, or all the cares of the world. It's easy to forget that the kingdom of heaven is near, is alive all around me. It is where I belong and where I am heading, and in the span of all eternity, I'll be going there soon. But I often forget this in the day-to-day grind of prayer needs.

However, the short-lived daisies make me stop and ponder the promise of heaven. When I see them, I sense God asking me, *Do you really believe all my promises are true?* He wants me to claim those promises for myself, not just generally assent to them in my mind. My Father wants me to cling to the promises of my inheritance in heaven now (Eph. 1:11, 14) as motivation to press on toward the goals he has waiting for me in the future (Phil. 3:14).

This is a treasure of blessings I often overlook. But when I have a visual cue to remember them, I am flooded with a new stream of peace and hope in a dry, neglected part of my heart. The freshness of the daisies reminds me to claim that heavenly hope for myself and experience greater peace and joy in the process. They prompt me to rejoice that Jesus is making all things new now, right in front of me on the country road.

Prayer

Father God,

I praise you for your promises of heaven. What a blessing it is to know you are preparing a place for me, a place with no tears or suffering, a place where your righteousness rules and all are safe in your loving presence.

I confess that I often lose sight of these promises. I intellectually accept them but personally forget to apply them. I consider them far off when you want me to hold them near. Forgive me for getting so caught up in daily life that I take my eyes off the many blessings you have in store, which you want to serve as incentives now.

Thank you for making all things new now, Jesus. Thank you for making all things new in the days to come when your justice and righteousness will reign and all will recognize you as Lord. Thank you for reminding me that the kingdom of heaven is right here with me when I choose to participate in the missions you place on my life.

Give me a heavenly mindset, Holy Spirit. Renew my mind with the truth of your Word, which can cause new life to grow in all the dried-up places of my thought life. I pray that as I choose to claim your promises now, I will experience greater hope, joy, and peace in my daily walk with you.

In Jesus's name,
Amen.

Reflection Questions

1. When you think of daisies, what ideas come to mind?

2. How often do you claim the promises of heaven for yourself?

3. If you chose to see yourself as an active participant in furthering God's kingdom every day, what difference could that make in your relationship with God and others?

CHAPTER FIFTEEN

COWS

For all the animals of the forest are mine,
and I own the cattle on a thousand hills.

Psalm 50:10 NLT

The cows grazing in the fields on my prayer walk always stir up good memories for me, not just for the meat they provide, which I love, but for good moments with extended family.

For many generations on my paternal side, my ancestors have been cattle farmers. I am blessed to be the oldest great-grandchild, and I also have a photographic memory, so I have treasured memories of butchering days when I was three years old.

While walking on my prayer walk route now, I can reflect on that day in early spring of 1981. It was chilly enough that I needed my light blue windbreaker, which I was proud to be able to zip up by myself. I was the shortest person in the group, except for my baby sister—at least I could walk around at elbow-level of all the adults and observe everything going on.

The men were outside—my grandpas, uncles, great-uncles, and all my dad's cousins. They were butchering the meat and hanging it up in the smokehouse. I was so curious, I ventured out into the place where they normally kept the tractors, whose front forks were hoisted high to hold the carcasses of cows and pigs. I smelled the fresh blood and sensed the reverence the men had for carving the meat from the animals they had tended for years. Even as a three-year-old, I sensed a holy feeling there of the animals' lives given to nourish all our lives. Deep respect abounded as the men worked mostly in silence.

Closer to the house, my great-grandfather was butchering chickens. He had a wonderful sense of humor and invited me to watch more closely. With a quick chop of his hatchet, he removed a chicken's head with hardly a drop of blood. But the dead chicken started chasing me! I can still hear his jolly laughter as I ran in circles, trying to avoid the headless monster. I ran inside where the ladies were seasoning hams and wrapping them in waxed paper. My great-grandmother was plucking feathers from the fattest hen, which she would soon cook into a pot of warm, delicious chicken and dumplings.

I know many people have never seen animals butchered, and some are squeamish about it, but I treasure this memory of butchering day. It happened before my parents divorced, and it speaks of the sense of community extended families are intended to give. The memory reminds me of our connection to the earth, animals, and other people. It causes me to praise God for the provision of meat for our food. This is something I never take for granted because I understand all the work that goes into caring for farm animals.

On my first and only trip to the West Coast in the late 1990s, I laughed at the marked-up price for "grass-fed beef" on restaurant menus. Every cow I encounter in southeast Missouri feeds on the grass of the fields, and I never knew that was a luxury item until I traveled outside this area. But ever since ancient times, cattle were the prized offerings at the temple, presumably because they required much more care and investment than the simpler sacrifices of grain or birds (Lev. 12:8).

I know not everyone eats meat, and I'm not trying to convert any of you to become omnivores. However, the Bible is clear that God provides cattle for food (Deut. 14:26), and he is the true owner of every cow that grazes on every pasture in the world.

Memphis is no longer afraid of the cows like he was as a pup. Instead, he respects them like I do, curiously watching them from the road. They are content to munch grass all day long, moving from field to field in their quest for sweeter-tasting greens. I am grateful for how well God provides for us through local farmers, whom we contact to get half a beef twice a year. The resulting meat turns into many delicious meals all year.

When I cook hamburger for dinner once a week, I remember that our meat is a gift from God. It is the work of many laborious hours of birthing; vaccinating; separating from mothers; herding from field to field; all the work involved in growing, cutting, raking, baling, and storing hay for the cows' food; shuttering in barns during cold weather; and finally, butchering. Many people have worked to put this two-pound package of ground beef together. I'm grateful to have watched that process come together with my own three-year-old eyes, and I still respect it today.

What a blessing to be reminded on all my prayer walks that God is providing my food through these animals. It's a blessing to remember that I'm connected to the people who tend these cattle and to the earth that feeds them. It's a blessing that reminds me God is in charge and opens his storehouses to provide the food I need.

Prayer

Father God,

I praise you for providing all the food I eat. It all belongs to you, and it all comes from you. I praise you for connecting me to the earth, animals, farmers, cooks, and grocers through my food.

I confess that I often overlook this important blessing. Without food, I couldn't survive. Without proper nutrition, I could not operate at my best potential in your kingdom service. Food is such a basic need that it's easy to take for granted, but I want to be more intentional in being grateful for my food and for all the hands that were involved in its preparation.

I thank you today for this abundant blessing of food. Thank you for providing for my needs in the food I ate today. May every bite of food be reason to praise you for your storehouses of blessing, Lord.

May I trust that since you own the cattle on a thousand hills, you will surely provide for all my needs. You will meet my needs for food, clothing, shelter, and more. May I never have an attitude of entitlement for these blessings, but may I appreciate that they come from your own hand as gifts to me.

In Jesus's name,
Amen.

Reflection Questions

1. What is your favorite food? How does it connect you to God, others, animals, and/or the earth?

2. When you think about God owning all the cattle in the world, what feelings stir in you?

3. If you took a reverent stance of gratitude for all the food you eat, how might it impact your faith?

CHAPTER SIXTEEN

MULLEIN

Give me neither poverty nor riches!
Give me just enough to satisfy my needs.
Proverbs 30:8b NLT

Everyone has a splurge item, whether it be food, clothing, jewelry, tools, or a host of other things. In the spring of 2020, I realized that one of my splurge items is a certain brand of toilet paper known for its cottony softness. Little did any of us know how much this household necessity would become yet another point of contention across the nation.

Right at the beginning of the pandemic, people were stockpiling toilet paper, although manufacturers emphasized the supply was intact. I heard that police were stationed at some stores to control hoarding, but I believe those were only rumors. Our local grocery store was stocking just a few packages of the cheap, non-cottony variety. Yet I was grateful to have whatever kind we could find, because we use up quite a bit as a family with three children.

Honestly, I had never given much thought to toilet paper until it was suddenly scarce. The only other time I considered it was when I read the dystopian classic *Alas, Babylon*, in which people greedily grabbed up flyers dropped from helicopters to substitute for toilet paper. During my reading of that novel, I would have never dreamed I'd face a toilet paper shortage in my lifetime. I did not go a day of 2020 without sufficient toilet paper, and I'm guessing that's true for most of us. Yet I began seeing toilet paper as a relatively modern luxury when I did some research into one of the plants along my prayer walk.

Each spring, a big, leafy plant with super fuzzy leaves caught my attention on the sides of the gravel road. When I touched the leaves, they felt as soft as cotton with their white, velvety surfaces. The plants grow in neat rosettes all year, and they then send up spikes with yellow flowers in late spring. My research told me these plants are named mullein, and they are highly valued for many purposes, both medicinal and practical. Native Americans may have used them for poultices, shoe or diaper linings, and yes, even toilet paper.[1]

Seeing the mullein rosettes on my prayer walks that spring made me smile. They helped me realize that God provides for all our basic needs, even the ones we usually don't consider. He cares about everything in our lives, including the most rudimentary requirements for our daily living. He knew that my family needed toilet paper and kept us supplied throughout quarantine because he loves us and cares for us in every way.

When I kept hearing about toilet paper shortages, I prayed for the people so consumed with fear that they compulsively hoarded a basic item. As I walked, I prayed for those who don't know God as their provider, the One who doesn't just cover the basics but gives in abundance. I asked God to help those seized with fear to turn to him with all their needs.

Fingering the soft mullein again, I thanked God for honoring our most modest parts by providing for them, not just those on our physical bodies, but the parts of the church body that often get overlooked (see 1 Cor. 12:21–26). Quarantine offered us the opportunity to see that all parts of the church matter—not only the pastors and worship team, but everyone who serves. Not too long ago, my pastors said there is a desperate need for greeters, workers in the nursery, and other less-heralded staff. At this writing, my church has not yet returned to fully functional status due to under-staffing in these more hidden, yet indispensable, roles of service. I'm sure that if this is true of my church, it is true of many others.

The humble mullein plant not only makes me think of the blessing known as toilet paper but also of the blessing of the entire body of Christ, known as the church. Every part matters, whether seen or unseen, whether presentable or offstage. The mullein reminds me to pray that more people will recognize their value in the body of Christ and connect with their local churches.

I pray the losses of quarantine will help us appreciate our day-to-day blessings more. I pray we won't be tempted to hoard, that we will not be so financially strapped that we cannot afford the basics of living. I pray we'll be satisfied with just enough to meet our needs, praise our provider for his gifts, and give back to the body of Christ in grateful service.

Prayer

Father God,

I praise you as the One who provides for all my needs, even the needs I overlook. You cover all the basics, and then you give me above and beyond that out of your abundance.

I confess that in stressful moments, I forget this truth and become fearful. In my fear, I can be tempted to hoard blessings, as if provisions depend on me alone. I need to trust that you will provide for me in all circumstances, giving me just what I need, somewhere between poverty and riches.

Thank you for teaching me about humility and dependence during quarantine. Thank you for opening my eyes to what I had been taking for granted. Thank you for teaching me what really matters in that time of testing.

Help me value what you value, Lord. May I serve you and your church out of gratefulness for all you provide for me. May I be ever satisfied with what you provide in my basic needs and in all the other opportunities you give me.

In Jesus's name,
Amen.

Reflection Questions

1. What feelings did shortages during the quarantine stir up in you?

2. Have you ever hoarded something due to fear? If so, how did this affect your relationship with God?

3. What role might you be willing to fill in your local church? If you aren't sure of your talents or strengths, take a free spiritual gifts test online to get some guidance, such as the test available at www.spiritualgiftsassessment.org/quiz.

NOTE

[1] Taylor Roatch, "The Only Plant That Should Be in Your First Aid Kit," *Ask a Prepper How to* . . . , April 27, 2017, http://www.askaprepper.com/plant-first -aid-kit/.

CHAPTER SEVENTEEN

DEAD TREE

*For Christ himself has brought peace to us. He
united Jews and Gentiles into one people when,
in his own body on the cross, he broke down
the wall of hostility that separated us.*

Ephesians 2:14 NLT

Some people move to the countryside to experience the quiet
peace of natural settings, to keep to themselves in respectful inde-
pendence. Others move to the country to embrace the wilderness,
to throw off the oppression of city living and its ordinances like
noise, burning, and mowing restrictions. Often, these two kinds
of people live side by side.

This is the story that comes to life each spring in my woods,
when all the trees sprout their fresh green leaves, except one: a
dead tree on the far northeast corner, with weathered gray claws
that permanently reach upward. Multiple species of woodpeckers
love this tree and relish the insects inside its decaying form. Yet
our neighbor wants it to come down.

This neighbor moved into the dwelling several years ago. Out
of all the neighbors who have lived there, his attitude is closest to

a bitter renegade. His patterns of behavior include booming late-night karaoke sessions, bullets pinging off our trees during target practice, dogs barking nonstop for fifteen hours in a row, a string of broken relationships, screaming matches full of expletives, whiskey bottles dumped at the edge of our pond, and burning toxins from his rusty trash barrel wafting straight into our ventilation system.

One winter afternoon a few years ago, I had had enough. I stomped down to the property line and confronted him in an act I have regretted ever since. After that failed attempt to reason with him, I resolved not to confront again unless it's a life-or-death situation.

A few months after that incident, I received a certified letter from the neighbor's attorney, curiously whited out in spots and fixed with blue ink, requesting the tree to be removed because it could result in property damage if it falls. That possibility exists, but I didn't deem it looming enough. The tree stands to this day, a symbol of years of conflict.

Unfortunately, this neighbor is distant kin to me, part of a branch of the extended family about whom many have said, "They think the rules don't apply to them." The fact that I share in this bloodline has challenged me over and over. For many years, I chose to put considerable distance between myself and the closest family member on that side due to the high toxicity level of the relationship. But I can't put that kind of physical distance between myself and my neighbor because we share a see-through, barbed-wire fence line.

I have long been fascinated with Robert Frost's famous poem, "Mending Wall," with which he opens, "Something there is that doesn't love a wall." Two neighbors in this country scene, who share a stone wall boundary, make repairs to their stone wall while seeing things from different perspectives. The narrator, an apple farmer, burns to tell his neighbor, "Something there is that doesn't love a wall, / That wants it down." Yet his neighbor, a keeper of pines, calmly states twice, "Good fences make good neighbors."

When I was in high school first encountering this poem, I took issue with the title. Why is it called "Mending Wall" when the poem displays so much consternation in the narrator's heart? Why isn't the title more about conflict, which would be more fitting? At the end, the narrator's opinion has grown bitter: "He moves in darkness as it seems to me, / Not of woods only and the shade of trees." Repairing the wall, side by side, seemed only to worsen the narrator's viewpoint.[1]

After my experience with a difficult neighbor, I think the title is not only appropriate, but hopeful. Sometimes I feel like the neighbor who calmly states the value of boundaries. Other times, my anger boils over, and my opinion grows darker. Only the act of mending holds hope, because if left to myself, I'll become embittered like my renegade neighbor.

I consider this poem every time I turn southward on my prayer walk, because I can clearly spy the dead tree on the far corner. I remember I am called to mend the wall between us as best as I can, as far as it depends on me (Rom. 12:18).

The mending I undertake looks mostly like prayer. I remember our commonality as children of divorce, and I humbly admit that I could be just as unhealed as him without God's intervention. I pray emotional and spiritual growth for him when I hear the ugly fighting in yet another one of his relationships tottering toward failure. I pray blessings and peace on him when I am tempted to grumble against the loud music, burning trash, and shattered whiskey bottles. When his dogs bark due to lack of attention, I pray for them, and I pray for my neighbor again.

Praying for him has softened my heart with compassion, although I doubt we will ever be reconciled. As I pound the gravel road on my prayer walk, I pray that God will break down the wall of hostility on my side and hopefully on his side as well. I pray that the dead tree will never fall over onto his property and that new life will grow on his side of the fence.

Prayer

Father in heaven,

I praise you for sending your Son, Jesus, to break down the walls of hostility between me and others. Without his sacrifice, I would never have peace in my relationships.

I confess that I am often a troublemaker in my heart. Although my actions may not show it, my thoughts do. You know my thoughts, and today I confess my angry, self-serving, judgmental, stubborn, and unloving thoughts against others. I ask you to cleanse me of these sins.

Thank you for teaching me to pray, forgive, and show compassion. I'm glad I don't have to mend walls all by myself because you will help me. I trust the Holy Spirit to show me exactly what I need to do to live in peace with everyone, even with my difficult neighbors.

Bear the fruits of the Spirit in me, especially the fruits of self-control, peace, and love. May the prayers over my difficult relationships soften my heart.

In Jesus's name,
Amen.

Reflection Questions

1. If you have had a difficult neighbor, what was that situation like? How did it bring out the worst and/or best in you?

2. Do you have a toxic family member? What does living in peace with this person, as far as it depends on you, look like in practical terms?

3. How might prayer change the most difficult relationship you have now? What reminder will you use to pray daily for this relationship?

NOTE

[1] Robert Frost, "Mending Wall," in *North of Boston* (London: David Nutt, 1914).

CHAPTER EIGHTEEN

HAWK

*And as Moses lifted up the bronze snake on a pole in
the wilderness, so the Son of Man must be lifted up, so
that everyone who believes in him will have eternal life.*

John 3:14–15 NLT

All year long, hawks scan the fields for rodents and other favorite
prey while I am on my prayer walks. These large birds keep their
distance from me and Memphis, yet I admire their strength and
persistence. They patiently wait in high tree branches with eyes
like sophisticated lasers, watching for the slightest movement in
the grass. If I were an animal in the fields, I would not wish to be
caught in a hawk's gaze, or worse, in its tight grasp or sharp beak.

Just one time on my prayer walks, I witnessed a spectacular
sight involving a hawk. Memphis and I were almost home, breathless from walking up the big hill toward our driveway. Right when
we drew near the cemetery, a hawk flew about forty feet in the air,
perhaps twenty feet south of us. A four-foot-long snake dangled
from its beak, and I could sense the hawk's relishing of its victory
in the confident set of its head and wings.

As you can imagine, this sight was a bit spooky. I don't like
seeing snakes anytime in my woods, although I'm well aware they

are always present. If they stay out of my way, I'm happy to stay out of theirs. One October afternoon, I almost stepped on a venomous copperhead because the brown leaves on the ground served as perfect camouflage. This past summer, when we had received a lot of rain and snakes were looking for dry places to rest, I came upon a black cottonmouth in our driveway. In another rainy season, I spotted a cottonmouth about ten feet in front of us on the gravel road, and I was relieved that Memphis didn't see it first since he would have strained to investigate. I turned him away, and we headed back home as fast as we could.

I am getting jittery just typing out my memories of these snakes. But truth be told, I am quietly thankful for their presence, because they do an excellent job of keeping the mice at bay. The mice drive us crazy with their midnight scrambling in our subfloors, nasty droppings in our storage rooms, and persistent foraging of bird seed. If the snakes reduce the load of mice, I'm all for them, as long as I don't have to see them in action.

That day on our walk, I could not help but look up at the snake. The hawk was flying away from us, not directly overhead, so I was not worried about the hawk dropping the snake on us. Instead, this odd sight transfixed me and strangely comforted me. It was as if I were seeing spiritual victory in action, and I needed that reminder.

In the Bible, serpents are associated with the devil and his evil companions (see Gen. 3 and Rev. 20:1–10). Also, in one Old Testament story, snakes were attacking people who were speaking out against God. When Moses sought a solution, God told him to make a bronze snake and put it on a pole, and anyone who looked up at the snake would be healed from their snakebites (Num. 21:4–9). The bronze snake held no power of its own. Instead, this was a foreshadowed symbol of Jesus nailed to a cross so that all who would look to him for help could be saved for all eternity.

When I saw the hawk carrying the snake, that Old Testament image immediately appeared in my mind, thanks to a past Bible Study Fellowship teaching. *Someday, God will make all things right.* He will declare the final victory against Satan and his evil agents. However, I am set free from bondage to evil because Jesus has rescued me for all time.

The spiritual battles I face often feel like vicious attacks from vipers who hide in the darkness and wait to strike me when I cannot see them coming. Seeing the snake that day reminded me that my spiritual battles are real. Believers must constantly be on guard against the evil forces that want to discourage us and take us down (see Eph. 6:10–18).

Yet I am not required to fight these battles on my own. My Savior is always watching me from above, scanning the battlefields in my mind and heart for trouble. He equips me to stand strong with the truth of his Word. He delivers me from evil and temptation when I cry out to him in prayer. I can always claim victory, even when the fighting is fierce, with God as my deliverer.

Now, when I reflect on when we saw the hawk carrying the snake, I find new resolve for my spiritual battles. I remember that God always watches me and will strengthen me for the fight. He will swoop down at just the right time to carry the evil one away from me, when I have passed the tests for his glory.

Prayer

Father God,

I praise you as my Savior, deliverer, rescuer, and redeemer. You deserve all praise for your omnipresence and omniscience. You never turn your eyes away from me, and you know all the difficulties I face.

I confess that I forget how you equip me to fight in spiritual battles. I get caught up in daily living and lose sight of my calling to stand firm in my faith against the temptations I face. I sometimes become discouraged by spiritual attacks, which wound my spirit. In these times, it's easy for me to forget you are always by my side.

Thank you for already securing the final victory against the devil and all forces of evil. Thank you for never leaving me alone in my spiritual battles. Thank you for equipping me to fight back in your strength, with your Word, and through prayer.

Empower me to put on your armor of protection so I can fight spiritual battles with greater resolve. Remind me to look up to you and cry out to you when I need help. I trust that as I turn to you in my battles, you will protect me from doubt and deliver me from evil.

In Jesus's name,
Amen.

Reflection Questions

1. What feelings come to mind when you think of hawks or snakes?

2. When have you felt like you were under attack by spiritual forces?

3. In what situation do you need God's deliverance? How can prayer help you trust God as your deliverer?

CHAPTER NINETEEN

HERON

Look at the birds. They don't plant or harvest or store
food in barns, for your heavenly Father feeds them. And
aren't you far more valuable to him than they are?

Matthew 6:26 NLT

Occasionally, I disturb a heron from its hidden place in the stream while I am prayer walking. Its presence is always a surprise and delight that encourages me.

Herons are one of the types of birds that I've seen on an irregular basis here in our woods. They always seem to arrive on a day when I'm feeling despondent, and I think God helps me see them on those down days so I'm lifted up. The heron is probably the most frequent visitor of the irregular visitors, and I happen upon it when I look out my wall of windows in the living room. It is always at the edge of the pond, peering patiently into the depths while perfectly balanced on one leg. The heron waits in calm stillness for an unsuspecting fish or frog to become its dinner. I have yet to see a heron strike at its prey, and I look forward to catching that glimpse someday.

Once, I saw a bald eagle dive down over our pond and grab a fish for its dinner. That was the most thrilling irregular bird visit to our property. More often, the wood ducks visit our pond and inspect it for a nesting area. How I wish this mated pair would build a nest in the high branches of our hard maples so we could watch their babies grow, but I think the nearby county road is too busy for their liking. On rare occasions, sleek Baltimore orioles will visit my bird feeders as they migrate through the area. They love snatching miniature fruits from the calamondin orange tree on my deck. They slice the oranges open with their scissor-like beaks and then lap the tart juice with their tongues.

These irregular bird sightings catch me off guard in the best way. I'm melancholy by nature, and I can get caught up in sad ruminations when I'm not mindful of my thoughts. But God uses these bird sightings to remind me he's right beside me, asking me to choose joy in every circumstance. The bird sightings provide a hard reset for my thought life motherboard, and I'm jolted back into the reality that I worship and serve a God who delights in good surprises.

That's why I love coming upon the heron in the spring, while it searches for fish in the stream. I never see it standing there, since the stream runs below ground level. Instead, I hear its wings flap as it rises between the trees, brushing the new spring leaves with its feathers. Once free from the woods, it glides in a silent flight, full of grace and peace. I watch as it flies low over the treetops, settling back into a northern part of the stream I never pass by on my walk. The heron is a smart bird, determined to locate its lunch in an undisturbed area.

The fact that all these birds display a dependence on God for their food source humbles me. Whether it's the eagle grabbing a fish with great aplomb, the wood ducks dipping below the surface of the pond to gobble up grub, the orioles sipping tangy orange juice, or the heron patiently waiting for a bullfrog to emerge, all of them display their utter dependence on God. They have nothing stored up in the woods for their food, like the squirrels who fill the rotted tree holes with acorns and hickory nuts. No, these birds live wing-to-beak, as I have sometimes lived hand-to-mouth. But they do this every single day in perfect peace, instinctively trusting their Creator to provide for them.

I can't count how many times I've been worried about money, and then an irregular bird arrival catches my eye right then. There have been times when I've been praying about provision, wondering how I could make the next payment, and a heron lifted from the stream at that very moment. It's as if Jesus is asking me again and again to look at the birds so I will trust him more, to see that I am far more loved and treasured than they are, so he will surely provide for all my needs out of the riches of his glory (Phil. 4:19).

Now, when I see the heron, I know God is speaking to me through its presence. He is calling me to patiently trust him as I wait for my provision to arrive. He wants me to fly forward with grace and peace, counting on him to lift me up. God wants me to take delight in the good surprises he has in store for me, not only cry out to him for help in my times of need. I'm always glad to see the heron on my prayer walk because it's a clear sign to reaffirm my trust in God.

Prayer

Father God,

I praise you as my provider. You care lovingly for the birds in your creation, and you care even more lovingly for me.

I confess that I often forget that you will provide for all my needs. I take my eyes off you and focus on my problems, worrying about how I will pay my bills or even how I will have enough to eat. Because you lavishly provide for my needs, it's a sin to doubt you in this area, and I confess it today.

Thank you for delighting in good surprises, Lord. Thank you for giving me reasons to choose joy every day even when I still have needs. Thank you that I can always name ten things for which I'm grateful, off the top of my head, because you are good to me.

Help me trust that you will provide for all my needs according to the riches of your glory, Jesus. Help me remember I worship the king who owns it all and is eager to share his goodness with me. When I see the birds, may it be a sign to remember that you provide all I need and more.

In Jesus's name,
Amen.

Reflection Questions

1. Which nature sightings inspire encouragement for you?

2. What financial needs do you wish were met today?

3. In what area do you need to trust that God has good and delightful surprises in store for you?

CHAPTER TWENTY

TOTALITY

When I consider your heavens,
the work of your fingers,
the moon and the stars,
which you have set in place,
what is mankind that you are mindful of them,
human beings that you care for them?

Psalm 8:3–4 NIV

I am incredibly blessed to have lived and to live in the path of totality for the solar eclipses of 2017 and 2024. My property is in the heart of the best viewing in the Midwest, where we can watch the sun and moon align for the longest period.

In August 2017, I had recently quit my day job to write full-time. For a few months, I had scrambled to find enough freelance work to equal what I had been paid as a high school secretary. By that time, I had settled into being a ghostwriter for criminal defense attorneys—not exactly what I wanted to do, but it paid well. I was working half as many hours for the same amount of pay, and I could officially call myself a writer. My dreams of writing for a living were beginning to come true.

But the dream to write books like this one wouldn't die. It was a fire burning inside me, and I desperately wanted to share that light with the whole world. I was spending all my time writing behind the scenes for other people. I wanted nothing more than to get a book contract, yet I didn't know how much more work I could add to my plate.

The day of the solar eclipse, I kept looking through my windows, waiting for things to change. The light was eerie, as in an Alfred Hitchcock movie. I drove on the country road to get up to the place where I wanted to watch this important event—the cemetery where my great-grandparents are buried, right across from our family farm, where the sky is wide open.

I trembled as the sky grew darker. I worried about where I would be in my life when the next eclipse occurred. What would happen with my writing dreams, my difficult marriage, the family farm, the broken relationships, and persistent struggles all around me? I pushed these worries to the side while the afternoon suddenly switched into evening.

Then, as the shadows aligned, I looked southward to see the sun obscured by the moon. I was speechless, although I heard "You Are the Sun" by Sara Groves on repeat in the background. Crickets and cicadas started singing. Cows mooed as they walked back to the barn. A bat flew past my head, thinking dusk had already arrived! The sun's blaze of light swirled around a pitch-black circle, and I stood marveling at God's undeniable glory displayed in a breathtaking two-minute, twenty-four-second span.

In my reflections after this event, I shared a thought with my email subscribers: "If God can align the sun, moon, and earth in a glorious display of his power, WHY am I still living in fear?"

I can't say that I've totally overcome fear now, years after the 2017 eclipse. I still have days when I worry about what life will be like when the next eclipse occurs in April 2024. But I've learned on my prayer walks, when I feel the afternoon sun shining on my skin, to surrender my fears to God, to remember that he was right by my side in 2017, to know he'll be right beside me again in 2024 and beyond, that he sees everything that will happen between now and then, and that he's trustworthy to guide and lead me through the unknowns.

It's good for me to reflect on that first day of totality during my prayer walks when I felt like such a small part of the universe in comparison to the spectacular event in the sky, when I realized how much I must mean to the One who makes the sun rise and set each day, who also cares lovingly for me, a tiny speck in all his creation.

When I was worried about many things, God was working all things together for my good, just as he is today (Rom. 8:28). He could see me taking prayer walks on these country roads, which I hadn't done before, with my Memphis who had yet to be born. He was at work behind all the scenes where I could not yet catch glimpses of his work. Some of the proof of his work is in this book you are reading right now—the third one that has been published since August 2017. I couldn't see my dreams unfolding then, but God saw them with perfectly clear vision.

How humbling. How inspiring. How encouraging. Those reflection times have been woven into many of my prayer walks, and I will keep weaving them in during the days to come. They are wonderful reminders to set my current worries and fears to the side and simply praise him as my marvelous Creator, echoing David's irrepressible worship: "LORD, our Lord, how majestic is your name in all the earth" (Ps. 8:9)!

Prayer

Father God,

I praise you as the Creator of all things, the sustainer of all life, the blessed controller of everything in heaven and on earth. You deserve all my praise and worship.

I confess that I often forget these truths and let my worries and fears overwhelm me. If I could only remember that you are watching over me just as you keep watch over all creation, what peace I could experience! Forgive me for steeping myself in fear and worry instead of immersing myself in worship and praise.

Thank you for the beauty of the sun, moon, stars, and skies. For your glory, they put on displays every day. Thank you for the reminders they quietly speak to me, to trust you as my Creator, sustainer, and blessed controller.

Help me to fully surrender all my worries and fears to you. Send me reminders in the skies that you have chosen me as a masterpiece of your creation, since I am made in your image. May I always be awed and humbled by the glory you display in creation, O Lord. May I ever be moved to praise you.

In Jesus's name,
Amen.

Reflection Questions

1. What feelings did you experience during the 2017 solar eclipse?

2. What worries and fears keep you from experiencing God's peace and block your praise and worship?

3. How might studying the skies both humble and encourage you?

SUMMER

CHAPTER TWENTY-ONE

HONEYSUCKLE

A person who is full refuses honey,
but even bitter food tastes sweet to the hungry.

Proverbs 27:7 NLT

In May, the wild honeysuckle bursts into bloom on the fence rows of the path I walk with Memphis. It also twines around some of the trees and covers part of the roadsides. The flowers smell so sweet I wish I could keep inhaling the scent instead of needing to exhale.

Honeysuckle smells like early summer to me. It's a signal of the perfect balmy weather in a two- or three-week window before the humidity and heat oppress us. I love sitting outside on my porch after a walk, taking in the lovely floral scent. When I was a child, I even drank the drops of sweet nectar from the base of the flowers.

However, from a gardening perspective, there are fewer plants I dread dealing with more than honeysuckle. This species of wild honeysuckle is not a native plant, and it aggressively spreads to crowd out other more respectful plants. The woody vines are difficult to remove with only garden gloves. No, I need sharp pruning shears and loppers to untangle it from my rock garden, compost pile, and flowerbeds.

Unfortunately, cutting it back or even spraying it with weed killer doesn't stop its spread. Its roots are the most aggressive part. Every little piece of root will sprout a new plant. You are better off digging the whole thing up, although it's impossible to know if you got every single root piece. I've been wrestling with honeysuckle for years in my gardens, and sometimes it wins the fight.

For several decades, I experienced a problem in my thought life that could be compared to honeysuckle. To cope with seasons of stress or feelings of loneliness, I would turn to fantasies during my afternoon naps. These fantasies were of the PG-rated, Hallmark movie variety. However, their irresistible scent held me captive for far too long before I took my problems to the counselor's office.

There, I discovered the reasons why I chose an escape route in the afternoons—that was the prime time for temptation for me as a latchkey child of divorce. After school was when I would indulge myself to cope with negative feelings I didn't know how to process as a child. I never imagined that fantasies I entertained in junior high would carry over into my adult life.

When you are hungry with unmet needs, even a fantasy world tastes good, at least for a little while. You forget that it leaves a bitter aftertaste, when you discover you feel even lonelier than before after reality inevitably returns. Then the cycle repeats, and you'll settle for tiny drips of honey because you are starved for attention and affection. Yet God is the only One who can fully fill your emptiness and satisfy your hunger.

That's why my problem was like honeysuckle. It took heavy-duty efforts to remove it from my thoughts, and the problem kept popping up even when I cleared all the obvious vines of my emotional issues. It took several years to dig out every root piece and put them in the burn pile where they belonged. I had to do this every time I was triggered by stress or loneliness.

With a lot of practice, prayer, and professional help, God enabled me to break free from this fantasy world. It no longer has a strong grip on me. However, I must vigilantly watch for it to pop up again, since I know Satan would love nothing more than to sow those wicked seeds in the good soil of my heart—the soil God has lovingly prepared for fruit bearing instead.

Now, each May, I thoroughly enjoy the scent of honeysuckle on my walk. But I also use that scent memory to thank God for setting me free from a thirty-year thought life problem. I ask him to search my heart again for any areas in which the vines are growing so I can pull them up before their stems grow woody and tough. I pray that they will never take such a hold on me again.

I also ask God to give me all the desires of my heart as I delight in him (Ps. 37:4). I have learned that when I express my deepest needs to him, like his peace when I'm stressed and his presence when I'm lonely, he is always eager to meet them. Unlike people, wonderful as they are, God is always available for me. He's ready to walk with me on our prayer walks, waiting to give me new insights, fresh hope, and renewed joy. When I turn to him with my triggers, he is always faithful to lavish his love on me.

How sweet those flowers are at first glance. How lovely the vines are on the fence rows, heavy-laden with honey-colored blooms each May. Their scent now prompts me to pray in ways to which I was totally blind years ago. How grateful I am for God's grace, which saves me from my sinful nature, especially in places no one else sees. How kind he is to remind me that I can get all my needs met in him first and then take them to people without needy clinging and desperate grabs for attention. He has healed me from the wounds that once cried out, and for that, I'm grateful.

Prayer

Father God,

I praise you for promising to meet all my needs. You are my comforter and friend, and I feel greater peace each time I draw near to you.

I confess that I do not always turn to you first when I feel stressed or lonely. I allow other substitutes to replace the love you offer. They always cause me to end up feeling even worse than before. I need your rescue from my unhealthy cycles.

Thank you for never leaving me alone, even when I forget you are beside me. Thank you for offering me forgiveness, grace, and a new path of obedience. Thank you for your offer to pull up each and every root of sin in my life.

Help me remember to call out to you for help when I feel stressed or lonely. May I no longer turn toward fantasies or cheap substitutes. May I fill myself first with the sweetness of your presence, so those bitter temptations don't seem as alluring.

In Jesus's name,
Amen.

Reflection Questions

1. What do you normally turn to when you feel stressed or lonely?

2. When has even bitter food tasted sweet to you, due to unmet needs?

3. What times of the day are best for you to fill up on God's presence, so you aren't as hungry for cheap substitutes?

CHAPTER TWENTY-TWO

THE PEACE OF WILD THINGS

The greater my wisdom, the greater my grief.
To increase knowledge only increases sorrow.

Ecclesiastes 1:18 NLT

In the summer of 2020, the whole United States seemed to be burning down in flames. I could hardly bear to watch the news or click on the trending Twitter hashtags. The brutal pandemic took a backseat to the injustice, riots, looting, and fiery chaos in several cities.

The culture was permanently shifting, just as the baby boomers I know have described the cultural shifts of their teen years. There would be no turning back, but I was barely grasping this new truth in June 2020.

A rusty 1994 Jeep Wrangler became a much-needed joyride for all of us in that difficult summer. We drove with the top down in the golden light of sunset, not only on the roads where I walk but on many more in the southwest corner of our county.

It was easy to pretend all was fine while we canvassed fields and valleys. We slipped back into comfortable nostalgia as we visited the historic covered bridge, and I reminisced about learning to drive in the 1990s. We passed neighbors on their porches and others out for an evening walk, and we waved hello to one another. Corn and soybeans peacefully grew on schedule in the fields, and pastures rested, having just been harvested for hay. If you hadn't turned on the news, you wouldn't have realized anything was different.

As much as I wanted to withdraw into this little protected bubble of my country property and the county roads and fields that surround it, I could not pretend any longer. I needed to vertically vent my own feelings of frustration and anger to God on my prayer walks, and I did so with hot tears and a few shouts of indignation. But I also needed to learn to listen in new ways, pray for my country like never before, and calm my spirit in God's presence.

One day, I simply didn't have the strength to walk or pray. I needed a self-care day to grieve and rest. I put on my flannel Snoopy pajamas I only wear in December, just to feel their softness against my skin. Memphis was my own therapy dog, and I petted him more than usual. My dear friend Brenda had sent me a care package of books and tea, and I sipped a hot cup of a new flavor while I read. I savored a square of Belgian dark chocolate more slowly than normal. The words of Psalm 10 jumped off the page, affirming my mix of emotions. I picked snow peas from the garden and a blue hydrangea for a vase on my dining room table. Finally, I opened my college copy of *Collected Poems* by Wendell Berry, and I read one of my all-time favorites: "The Peace of Wild Things."

Berry published this poem in 1968, another year when our culture was on fire. This poem in my book is separated by one page from another poem, "Against the War in Vietnam." I felt that same slow-burning sense of injustice in me and the same overwhelming desire to throw myself into God's arms via nature. The poem was a welcome balm to my sorrow.

In this poem, which I highly encourage you to read online, Wendell Berry observes the pond where a wood duck and heron visit, much like my own pond. He muses on the animals' inability to worry about coming grief and how that fact imbues peace to them. Visiting the pond helped him find a moment of freedom from his worry, fear, and even despair for his children's future. Nature is where he reconnected with God and where his mental reset occurred.

During that difficult month, I reread his poem again and again, along with psalms of lament. On my prayer walks, I entered observer mode, to which I default when I'm under tremendous stress. The cows still chewed grass and cooled themselves in the stream. The birds still flew and sang and chirped. The bullfrogs still bellowed their summer love songs. Leaves still swayed in the warm southwestern winds. Wildflowers still opened their faces to the sun. Indeed, nature was not taxed by grief like I was, because it instinctively knows God is in full control. This fact was a great comfort to me in my heartsickness.

Since we are made in the image of God, we will experience grief and sorrow, unlike the rest of nature. However, in his infinite grace and kindness, God has provided the beauty and constancy of nature as an elixir when our hearts are sick with too much knowledge about evil. I'm ever grateful that God met me on that country road in June 2020, holding me while I showed him how heartbroken I was for my nation. He also used that time to set me on a regular praying assignment for the future of the United States.

As he increases my wisdom and knowledge through Spirit-led prayer, he also invites me to give my grief and sorrow over to him rather than slipping back into nostalgia. He also gives me the beautiful balm of nature as a salve for my open wounds, which he lovingly applies during my prayer walks.

Prayer

Father God,

I praise you for your wisdom and knowledge. You know all things, including all the events in the world before they occur. You set me in this specific time and place according to your perfect wisdom.

I confess that I do not always handle grief well. I get stuck in denial, anger, and sadness. I even try to avoid grief by longing for the old times. But none of this moves me forward in the path to which you call me. I need your help walking through the steps of grief so I can receive healing and hope.

Thank you for making me in your image, which includes experiencing wisdom and knowledge with grief and sorrow. Thank you for the constant balm of nature, which can refresh my spirit when my world feels chaotic.

Help me to trust you during the changes in culture. May your Holy Spirit help me practice self-control so I respond rather than react. May I learn to listen, pray, and calm myself in your presence when I am frustrated and worried. Empower me to be an agent of peace and light in the face of evil.

In Jesus's name,
Amen.

Reflection Questions

1. What emotions did you experience in the summer of 2020?

2. How have you handled grief in the past? How would you like to learn to handle it differently?

3. How could experiencing nature bring you closer to God and help reset your mindset?

CHAPTER TWENTY-THREE

DAYLILIES

*And why worry about your clothing? Look at the
lilies of the field and how they grow. They don't
work or make their clothing, yet Solomon in all his
glory was not dressed as beautifully as they are.*

Matthew 6:28–29 NLT

Every June, the daylilies open on the roadsides. These orange
flowers aren't native to Missouri, but I love them all the same. They
fill the road banks with color and delight.

These flowers always remind me of two things. First, they
bloom right in time for my middle child's birthday. I remember
putting him in a sling when he was only a few days old to go pick
a bouquet with his two-year-old brother. Now that they are both
teens, this is a precious memory of mine.

The other thing these flowers remind me about is Father's Day.
In high school, I cooked my first entire meal from scratch as a gift
to my father on that day, based on a menu I found in a women's
magazine. I set a huge vase of daylilies and Queen Anne's lace on
the table for the occasion, picked from the roadsides. These flowers have graced my table every Father's Day since then.

On my prayer walks, I enjoy their orange glory, which lasts only one day. Since there are multiple flowers on each stem, the bloom period lasts for weeks, yet each individual flower only opens for about sixteen hours. This is a sharp contrast to many other wildflowers and cultivated flowers I have seen or grown, which hold their blooms for several days or weeks.

The daylilies remind me most of Jesus's teaching about flowers. We don't know exactly which flowers he referred to in Matthew 6:28–29. He probably waved his hand to gesture toward whatever flowers were growing near him and the crowds, so the people had a live word picture while he spoke. Perhaps he used the generic term *lilies* to make this lesson applicable in all parts of the world, in all seasons, for all people.

His audience would have fondly reflected on the days of Solomon when there was peace and prosperity for the kingdom of Israel. Those were the glory days for God's people, when all twelve tribes lived in safety with plenty to eat (1 Kings 4:25), the days when workers kept busy building a glorious temple for the Lord rather than fighting wars, because Solomon's father, David, had defeated all their enemies (1 Kings 4:24).

King Solomon was known for his wisdom and his vast wealth. I imagine Hebrew parents telling their children stories about his beautiful robes and possessions, which even the Queen of Sheba admired (1 Kings 10). He was the king who brought the Ark of the Covenant into the temple and united God's people (1 Kings 8). The peak of his rule was the peak of ancient Israel's history, and it's safe to say that all the Jews in Jesus's time longed for those days to return.

I think Jesus chose Solomon to illustrate his truth for a special purpose. He knew his fellow Jews were hard-pressed by heavy Roman taxation, so they worried about the clothes they would wear and the food they would eat. He knew they would long for the days of Solomon again, when no one worried about what they would wear. Everyone had enough, and all was right in the world for a time.

Although I don't worry about having enough clothes now, there have been times when our clothing budget was super tight, times when all I could afford was secondhand or clearance items. I remember meditating on Matthew 6:25–33 in those days, praying that God would provide more clothes for my family. He has been faithful to provide enough clothing for me and my family during and since those hard times, just as he was faithful to the Jews during Jesus's time.

Few of us wear clothes only one time unless they are for a special occasion. Most of us need clothes that will last for a long time. But flowers like daylilies are gorgeous for one single day, like a bridal gown. They beautifully reflect God's glory, just like Solomon did in his royal robes. No one can create a single atom of a daylily from scratch like God does, yet he chooses to lavish his provision on these flowers that live only one day. He will also provide us clothing that lasts longer than the beauty of a daylily—plenty of clothing to keep us warm, dry, and stylish.

In quarantine, I learned how little I needed new clothing. I learned to appreciate what was already in my closet, because I couldn't add to it for a time with the stores being closed. That lesson, along with Jesus's teaching, helped me value my clothes even more. I may not ever be dressed as beautifully as Solomon, but I don't need to be. I can look at the daylilies on my prayer walk, appreciate their short-lived beauty, and remember that one of the ways God faithfully cares for me is by clothing me every day.

Prayer

Father God,

I praise you for providing clothing for me. I not only have what I need, but I also have some items just for pleasure. What a blessing it is to have my own racks and drawers filled with the clothes you provide, Lord!

I confess that I forget this basic blessing. Sometimes I worry about not having enough to wear. Other times I don't appreciate the clothes I have. Still other times, I crave more clothes that I don't need. This is an area where I need your guidance, Lord.

Thank you for every piece of clothing I own. Thank you for clothing the flowers so beautifully for my enjoyment. Thank you for teaching me simple lessons about my blessings through nature.

Help me appreciate the clothes that I own. May I trust you to provide any additional clothes that I need. May I be intentional in giving away or selling the clothes I don't need, so others may benefit from them. May I be prudent in what I add to my clothing collection to be a good steward of your resources. May the clothes I wear reflect your glory, Lord.

In Jesus's name,
Amen.

Reflection Questions

1. What is your favorite article of clothing, and why?

2. When have you worried about not having enough clothes? When have you underappreciated the clothing that you had?

3. What lessons did you learn about clothing during quarantine? How can those lessons help you live with greater trust and gratitude now?

CHAPTER TWENTY-FOUR

QUEEN ANNE'S LACE

Let us rejoice and be glad and give him glory!
For the wedding of the Lamb has come, and
his bride has made herself ready.

Revelation 19:7 NIV

June is traditionally wedding season, and it's also when the Queen Anne's lace blooms in profusion along my prayer walk. They line the gravel roads like decorations for a wedding, and they put me in a celebratory mood.

The white flowers are members of the carrot family. They are technically weeds because their seed heads spread their kind freely, but I consider them some of the most beautiful wildflowers on my walk. Their lacy heads sometimes span four or five inches across. I love taking them in my hands and admiring the hundreds of tiny white petals on a single stem.

These flowers are long-lasting in bouquets, a perfect contrast to short-lived daylilies, which bloom at the same time. They also dry well, and I enjoy pressing them for crafts. Since everyone seems to enjoy their carefree beauty, I love working their designs into my artistic creations.

Lace is often used in weddings. My own wedding dress was completely covered in lace, with sequins and pearls sewn on for decoration. The intricate patterns of Queen Anne's lace flowers remind me of the lace I chose for my dress. The flower festoons on both sides of the road make me feel like I'm walking up a wedding aisle again.

Although all other religions ask us to perform to win a god's approval, Jesus extends an intimate invitation to relationship, and he's already paved the way for intimacy through his sacrifice on our behalf. The church is a bride being prepared for her bridegroom, Jesus. All believers for all time make up the church, and imperfect though we may be, Jesus sees us through eyes of love. He wants nothing more than for us to be united with him in heaven, and he's preparing a giant wedding banquet for us to enjoy once evil has been banished forever (see Rev. 21 and 22).

When I see the lacy flowers lining the gravel road, I am amazed at the intimacy of relationship to which Jesus calls me. He doesn't only want to hear my requests; he wants my heart, mind, body, spirit, soul—everything. What I have found in my walk with God is that the door to a deep, meaningful relationship with God is obedience. Once you give yourself fully to him, like a bride gives herself to her groom or a groom gives himself to his bride, he rewards your obedience with powerful, mysterious intimacy. There is no other way to achieve this depth of faith. But the rewards are sweet and worth every sacrifice I've ever made, and I'm blessed beyond measure to have an intimate faith relationship with him.

The June flower profusion also reminds me that Jesus wants nothing more than for me to be united with the rest of the body of Christ, his church. For me, this pursuit seems much more difficult than pursuing intimacy with Jesus. However, it's not one or the other—the two most important commandments are to love God and love others (Matt. 22:37–40). As challenging as those commandments are, I must pursue them fully to show my love and devotion to God. He's stretching me and shaping me while I put on more beautiful attitudes toward others in the church, even when we don't agree or while I'm still healing from a wound caused by a fellow brother or sister in Christ.

Queen Anne's lace is pure white, reminding me that when the church is finally united for Christ, it will be cleansed and made holy by the blood of his sacrifice. There will be no more misunderstandings, arguments, judgments, divisions, grudges, or spiritual abuse. There will be no more wolves in sheep's clothing, weeds among the wheat, or false prophets. Only those who are fully committed to the Lord, no longer burdened by our sins in heaven, will be the bride. What a beautiful ceremony that will be! What a blessed celebration banquet!

My calling now is to be sanctified, day by day, in preparation for the bridegroom's arrival. Meeting him on the prayer walks to confess my sins and ask for his guidance helps me pursue sanctification. I want to be set apart for his glory, pure white like the lacy flowers that line the wedding aisle for his arrival.

Prayer

Dear Jesus,

I praise you as my bridegroom, the One who pursues me with relentless love, the king who longs to hold me close in a warm, intimate embrace.

I confess that I resist this intimacy with you. Sometimes I forget your grace and pull away from you in shame, not wanting you to see the real me. Other times, I let bad things or even good things become substitutes for the intimate love only you can provide. Forgive me for my divided heart.

Thank you for being the only God who makes a personal relationship possible. I don't have to do anything to earn your affection because you have already paid the price for me. I simply need to draw close to you, and you will draw close to me. Thank you for the privilege of this intimacy with you.

Give me courage to open more of myself to you. Help me relax in your love. May I find more riches of relationship with you as I pursue greater obedience in loving you and loving others, especially in the church.

In your name I pray,
Amen.

Reflection Questions

1. What is the best wedding you've ever attended or participated in, and why?

2. How would you like to grow in your relationship with God?

3. Which areas, whether disobedience, fear, shame, or something else, may be blocking a more intimate relationship between you and God?

CHAPTER TWENTY-FIVE

MILKWEED

The eyes of all look to you,
and you give them their food at the proper time.
You open your hand
and satisfy the desires of every living thing.

Psalm 145:15–16 NIV

In mid-June, the milkweed plants send their shoots up to attract pollinators. I see their light mauve globes with many bracts blooming on stalks about four feet high along the gravel road. On one side of the road near our woods, a rare white milkweed grows in the shade, and on the other side, there is a stand of deep magenta-colored milkweed plants. In my own flowerbed, I've planted yellow and orange milkweed for a specific purpose.

Milkweed is the favorite food of monarch butterflies. I have learned in gardening seminars at my local nature center that monarch numbers are on the decline. They overwinter in a specific region of Mexico, where their habitat is threatened. But if those of us who live between Mexico and Canada will grow more of their favorite plants, we can help sustain and boost the monarch population.

I once watched a television show that said a monarch butterfly that visits my Midwestern garden in June could be a great-grandchild of a butterfly who left Mexico. Then, a monarch who passes back through here in September could be a great-grandchild of a Canadian butterfly. The milkweed here could potentially feed several generations of these short-lived creatures. I'm happy to help with my own plants, and I'm thrilled to see so many wild milkweed plants on my prayer walks.

In my studies on native plants, I've learned that they are timed to bloom right when their favorite pollinators pass through the planting area. This is the reason most flowers bloom for only a few weeks at a time—they are feeding stations for migrating or recently hatched pollinators. Some flowers open only at night to attract moths who have bodies perfect for pollinating those exact flowers. There is no way this happens by accident. Only our magnificent Creator could keep all the bloom times straight, so all his creatures are fed.

When I think of the distance a tiny butterfly must travel and all the challenges she faces on her journey, I am amazed at God's provision. God cares enough about this species of butterfly to cause milkweed plants to grow in the right places and bloom at the right times. He knows that they seek this particular plant species for food, and they pass through this route year after year, so he makes sure the plants grow right where the butterflies will find them.

Sometimes I see monarchs on my prayer walks, and they always give me hope. Whether I see them flying free over the fields or feeding on the milkweed, I praise God for feeding all his creatures with such intention. He is kind to keep all the animals and insects fed, never overlooking the smallest details. This knowledge overwhelms me with a desire to praise him. He cares about this particular butterfly's part in its family history, so he must surely care for the details in my life.

These monarch butterflies help me remember that God times all his provisions of food for me too. He provides food for me several times a day, right when my blood sugar is low, and I need a calorie boost. The Holy Spirit gives me specific Bible verses at just the right time so I can be encouraged in a certain area or share a verse with a friend who needs it that day. He also directs me to blog posts, books, podcasts, sermons, and Christian songs to teach and comfort me on specific issues with which I am struggling. I can't count how many times God has used people to smile at me, strike up conversation with me, listen to me, or give me a hug exactly when I need it. In all these ways, he opens his hand to feed me and satisfies my needs.

He does this most frequently on my prayer walks, feeding my spirit with his affirmation, guidance, correction, and love. I'm thankful that when I spy a monarch butterfly on my prayer walks, I'm reminded of God's perfect timing in meeting my needs.

Prayer

Father God,

I praise you for your perfect timing. You feed all your creatures at the proper time, and you feed me too. I praise you for opening your hand to me to satisfy my desires.

I confess that I sometimes don't trust you to provide at just the right time. At times, I struggle with doubt that you know what is best for me. Other times, I jump ahead of you and choose my own timing instead of yours. Forgive me for letting my fear, doubt, and impatience get in the way of a deeper trust in you.

Thank you for perfectly timing everything for my good. Even when your answers do not match my preferred schedule, I know that you have the best in mind for me. Thank you for reminding me that if you provide so well for a butterfly, surely you will provide for me at just the right time.

Help me reflect on situations when your timing was ideal for me. May I be patient and trusting in a current situation that depends on your timing. May I trust you more each day as I wait for you to provide in the future.

In Jesus's name,
Amen.

Reflection Questions

1. What fact about a butterfly's life is most interesting to you?

2. When has God's timing been perfect in your life?

3. Which desires do you need to trust God to satisfy?

CHAPTER TWENTY-SIX

SUNBEAMS

How great you are, Sovereign LORD!
There is no one like you, and there is no God but you,
as we have heard with our own ears.

2 Samuel 7:22 NIV

In late June 2019, God gave me a hopeful vision one early morning. It came to me through perfectly timed sunbeams.

Memphis was only six months old and chock-full of energy. As soon as the sun rose at 5:41 a.m. that Sunday morning, he wanted to devour his food and then go on a walk. I am a morning person, but I wasn't all that excited about his early morning energy burst. Still, that's what comes with the territory when you have a new puppy.

I was groggy due to not sleeping well the night before. My mind was full of stimulation from an event on Saturday night, and I was still processing it. I heard Memphis whining at my bedroom door but tried to stay in bed as long as possible. Finally, his whining got on my nerves. I got up, threw on some clothes and my walking shoes, pulled my hair up into a messy ponytail, and opened the door to a very lively pup.

Normally, I eat my peanut butter toast, slowly sip my cup of hot tea, and read my Bible while Memphis gnaws on a rawhide treat after his breakfast. But that morning, he was raring to go on a walk. I gobbled down a banana, grabbed his leash, and headed out into the beautiful yet slightly foggy morning.

Memphis pulled me up the driveway, and God began speaking healing words to my heart. As we walked down the hill toward the gravel road, I rubbed sleep out of my eyes while God spilled out promises about the future in an encouraging, prophetic voice.

We started walking on the gravel road right when the sun rose above the horizon. The ground is low there, and the fog was thicker. Right when Memphis and I neared the gate at the top of the gravel hill, dozens of sunbeams broke through a stand of trees, cutting through the fog in a picture-perfect display.

God stopped me there. He told me to secure that picture of sunbeams in my mind. He instructed me to save it as a memory to pull up when I experience fear or discouragement about the future. He said it is a visual symbol of the redemption and restoration he is working in the days to come, and I could pull it up in my memory anytime I needed it.

Memphis had been wiggly that morning, but he sat still for several moments to gaze at the sunbeams beside me. I felt like I needed to take my shoes off, since I was obviously in a holy place (Exod. 3:5). But I was so overcome with joy, hope, and peace in that moment, I simply stood there in silence, soaking it all in.

Without question, that was the most powerful moment of all my prayer walks. It's rare and beautiful to hear God speak promises about my future. I don't go on prayer walks hoping to receive words like that every day. They are special treasures I don't deserve, yet ones I hold close in my memory.

What I've reflected on most often when I remember that incident is God's sovereignty. This characteristic of God means he sees the past, present, and future from a single vantage point, because he is infinite. His sovereignty also connotes a peaceful and powerful headship over all things. It's one of the most comforting aspects of God that often inspires my praise.

I have often thought about God's sovereignty on that Sunday morning—how he worked every little thing together for my good. He timed the sunbeams at the right moment, when I would fully absorb their beauty for a few minutes before the fog lifted. To get me on that road at the right moment, he gave Memphis extra energy to propel us outside faster than normal. If I had eaten my regular breakfast or taken any additional time getting ready, I would have missed the full glory of the sunbeams.

I have pulled up that picture in my mind many times when fear and discouragement have tempted me. The sunbeams only lasted a few minutes, yet they live on in my memory. I'm grateful that God gave me a special dispensation of his grace that morning, speaking hope to me through his light. Every time I've seen a sunbeam since, I praise him for his sovereignty over my life now and in the days to come.

Prayer

Father God,

I praise you for your sovereignty. There is no one like you, and there is no God but you, who can see past, present, and future all at one time. How great you are, sovereign Lord!

I confess that I often fall prey to fear or discouragement rather than trusting that you are in control of every detail of my life. It's tempting to worry about the future. Yet your promises are true, and you are faithful. Forgive me for losing sight of your unchanging character, Lord.

Thank you for working every little detail together to show me your glory and grace. Thank you for preparing good things in the future for me. Thank you for upholding me in every moment.

Open my eyes to the promises you have for my future, Lord. Help me trust that you have joy, hope, and peace in store for me. Drive out my fear and discouragement with your comfort and encouragement. May I trust that you are working all things together for my good.

In Jesus's name,
Amen.

Reflection Questions

1. In which situation has God worked many details together for your good at just the right time?

2. What hope does God want you to have for your future?

3. Which picture can you pull up in your mind to remember God is sovereign in your life?

CHAPTER TWENTY-SEVEN

STORM

When the storms of life come, the wicked are whirled
away, but the godly have a lasting foundation.

Proverbs 10:25 NLT

On one summer evening, I almost got caught in a thunderstorm. I did not check the weather forecast before heading out after supper, and I couldn't see the threatening clouds from our woods. A prayer need stirred in me, and I headed out into the oppressive summer humidity, determined to work out my situation in prayer.

This plan progressed well until I reached the gravel road and the open sky. I saw a wall of dark clouds heading toward me from the southwest. Thinking I would only get rained on, I foolishly reasoned I could finish my walk, which was almost halfway over. I kept pouring my prayers out while I walked northward toward the bridge.

When I turned around at my halfway point, I saw lightning flashing high in the towering cumulonimbus. Loud thunder startled me and the cows, who were running for shelter under a tree line. The clouds were speeding in the sky, so I picked up my pace. I hate running, but walking was no longer the safest option. I needed to get back to my property as fast as possible, but I needed to travel on the open gravel road first, where lightning strikes threatened.

While I jogged, I prayed that God would protect me from the lightning. I saw bolts flashing downward then, not too far away, according to the close thunderclaps. Normally, I am careful to a fault, so I spoke some harsh words to myself in between panting for breath. I spotted a wolf spider nearly as big as my hand running across the road in front of me, and I shuddered, thinking it was a bad omen.

However, God helped me run fast enough to get home before the thunderstorm was overhead. I was soaked from warm, fat raindrops that fell once I reached the paved road, but I was relieved and thankful to be safely home.

Ever since that scary evening, I have not headed out for a prayer walk when another storm is threatening. However, the memory of this particular prayer walk is deeply impressed in my memory because it taught me to turn to God first when I am afraid for my physical safety. I'm not often in such threatening situations, but when I feel uneasy about a perceived threat, I can immediately turn to God in prayer and experience a stronger feeling of his comforting presence.

We learn in Psalm 55:22 that as we give our burdens over to God in the storms of life, he will care for us and keep us from slipping and falling. This doesn't mean I will never take a tumble on the gravel road if another storm presses upon me, nor does it mean that I will never experience problems within other storms of life. Yet it does mean that God is able to handle my burdens better than I can. He promises to care for me no matter what storms I face and to watch over every step I take, preventing me from the worst falls.

It's easy to take my peace of mind for granted until the storms of life threaten to wreck it. What a blessing it is that God provides a lasting foundation for me in the storms of life, so I can turn back to him and experience the peace of resting on it again. I try not to take this blessing of peace for granted, and the storms of life remind me how precious it is.

On my prayer walks, I often consider people I know who do not seem to have the peace of the Lord in their hearts. No wonder they are so frightened in the storms they face. No wonder they cling to the things of the world when they feel threatened. They have yet to experience the perfect peace that surpasses all understanding, which can guard their hearts and minds in Christ Jesus (Phil. 4:7 ESV). I remember to pray that God will reach them in their fears, and they will turn toward him as a trustworthy Father.

I also pray for fellow Christians who are more prone to worry than the rest of us. I know a few who truly struggle with fears when the storms of life batter them. They are believers, but their fears drag them downward. In my prayers, I ask God to lift them up and help them realize the firm foundation beneath their feet. I pray they will not fear being whirled away in the storm, because God is upholding them with his "righteous right hand" (Isa. 41:10 NIV). Then as I walk back home, I ask God to remind me that his righteous right hand is also holding me up in the storms I face, strengthening and helping me along the way.

Prayer

Father God,

I praise you for protecting me in the storms I've faced. Whether literal or figurative, you have always stood by my side, shielding me from the worst blows. Only you can do this, Lord, and you deserve all the praise.

I confess that I often let my fears overtake me during storms. I panic and run to the things of the world instead of trusting that you are always by my side. Remind me that I can lean on you and take shelter in your refuge when the storms of life assail me.

Thank you for keeping me from slipping and falling when I give my burdens to you, Lord. Thank you for promising the peace that surpasses all understanding to me, even in the middle of the worst storms I may face.

Help me remember former storms through which you carried me so I can trust you more in the future storms I will face. May I take comfort in the fact you are upholding me in your righteous right hand, and may I also encourage others with this truth in their storms.

In Jesus's name,
Amen.

Reflection Questions

1. What is the scariest storm you have ever faced in nature and in life?

2. How have you experienced God's protection in past storms?

3. Who needs your encouragement in a current storm, and what will you do to reach out to them?

CHAPTER TWENTY-EIGHT

LITTER

Night is the time when people sleep and drinkers get drunk. But let us who live in the light be clearheaded, protected by the armor of faith and love, and wearing as our helmet the confidence of our salvation.

1 Thessalonians 5:7–8 NLT

They multiply every summer, all the way down the hill on both sides. Beer cans, glass bottles, multiple emptied fifths of vodka and bourbon and tequila. The people who are buying them must be purchasing them from convenience stores nearby, not the dressier grocery stores. These containers are the cheapest ones on the shelves. There are scores of them on my mile-and-a-half walk, some whole, some smashed. I should pick them up and recycle or throw them away. I even have a long-handled grabber that was one of my children's toys, which would be perfect for this dirty job. Yet I cannot bring myself to touch them.

When I first started these walks, I noticed all the litter. A recovering perfectionist, I visually separated the Styrofoam cups, potato chip bags, and fast-food trays with scorn from the natural landscape. *Who doesn't know better? Don't be so selfish and lazy.*

Take it inside, my inner critic would snarl at unidentified offenders. These prayer walks around litter often bring my judgmentalism up to the surface for confession.

But this particular litter of alcohol containers stirred up indignant anger in me. "Breaking the law, drinking, and driving. Probably underage," I muttered under my breath, though no one was around to agree with me. Then, suddenly, I pictured my oldest son's peers, mere freshmen and sophomores in high school, pausing to wonder if the underage drinkers who dump alcohol containers on this road took algebra or history alongside him, ate lunch in the same cafeteria, dressed out for the same PE classes, or rode the same school buses. This thought saddened me, as I realized they could easily be my own sons, my own daughters.

I chose to view the empty aluminum cans and brown beer bottles as a call to pray. At first, it was a prayer only for my children's faceless peers, partying in their cars and trucks on hot and humid Friday and Saturday nights, those who tossed their spent cans and bottles on the roadside to hide evidence, although Missouri is one of a handful of states with no prohibition on open containers in vehicles. I prayed they would come to yearn for God's love so deeply that their thirst could only be quenched with his living water.

And after I prayed for them, the trash became personal, manna meant to be a mirror.

I have never lived a day of my life untouched by alcohol, not by my own use, but by my loved ones' overuse. Until I attended Al-Anon in 2019, I had not realized how far it reached into my life. In my family, alcohol has ruined marriages, families, parties in the park, bonfires, trips to St. Louis Cardinals games, fancy banquets, regular weeknights, and much more.

One winter afternoon at my group meeting, it was my turn to share. At that time, a trend was hot on Facebook—share two photos, ten years apart, side by side. I searched my journals for winter 2009 entries and was stunned and saddened to view my report through newly recovered eyes. That year, I was scrambling to prepare for the arrival of an ice storm. In 2008, a severe ice storm had knocked out our power for three days, and I did not want to be unprepared again. Working at a feverish pace all day, I washed, cleaned, cooked, and poured water into every open drinking container. This water was reserved for toilet flushing and hand washing, because when our power goes out, so does our well pump. I had worked and worked to fend off the fury of another ice storm, but, of course, the storm arrived anyway.

Verbally processing this memory in my group, I drew a correlation. All my life, I had worked and worked to keep alcohol from seeping in. I told myself it may affect *them*, but not me. But I came apart when I admitted my realization: alcohol had seeped into every crevice I thought I had kept bone-dry through isolation, self-righteousness, and religious fervor. It had even invaded my secret thought life, which enraged me. I was dripping wet, soaked to the core with its damage. Yet I also felt as empty as a crushed aluminum can lying on the side of the road.

That litter—that cast-off, no-name cheap vodka bottle— became manna with my name on it, the manna of God's provision, because by his grace alone, I did not succumb to my DNA-encoded pathway toward addiction. Perhaps I unknowingly live a story today a mere three choices away from riding these exact country roads in the middle of the night the summer of my sixteenth year, bingeing on alcohol to fill up my desperately empty love tank. Instead, God had mercifully set me apart—manna for humble praise.

The litter was also a reminder to keep praying for my loved ones still bound in slavery to their addictions: prayers of compassion, since I had already processed my rage, indignation, and sorrow at Al-Anon; prayers for persistence in the fight, because signs of improvement can be slow to appear and because my own recovery is also long and complicated; and prayers for my own healing, asking God to use his supernatural shop vacuum to clean up every drop of the mess alcohol has made in my life.

I have yet to pick up a can or bottle from the roadside. For now, they are my manna markers. They are reminders to pray not only for the faceless, but for the faces I know and love. To persevere in prayer each day, I see this manna lying on the grass, like dew from heaven.

Prayer

Father in heaven,

I praise you for your holiness. Nothing escapes your notice, not even the voids I hold inside, which only you can completely fill.

I confess the inappropriate ways I have tried to fill up my voids, when all you wanted me to do was draw closer to you in my loneliness, hurt, and anger; and the many ways I have binged on the world instead of feasting on the manna of your loving presence.

Thank you for setting me apart for your glory, for keeping me from falling into greater sin, for guarding choices I could have made, only three steps away from a totally different life, far from you. Thank you for choosing me.

May I walk in the light, forsaking the darkness. May you give me a clear mind, protecting me with spiritual armor, giving me confidence in my salvation. May you soften my heart toward the addicted. Show me how to invite them to drink your living water.

I lift this prayer up in the name of Jesus,
Amen.

Reflection Questions

1. Does litter irritate you? Why or why not?

2. How could a piece of litter potentially reveal a sin in your life?

3. What pieces of litter will be the most useful tools in your prayer life?

CHAPTER TWENTY-NINE

PLANTAIN WEED

You cause grass to grow for the livestock
and plants for people to use.
You allow them to produce food from the earth—
wine to make them glad,
olive oil to soothe their skin,
and bread to give them strength.

Psalm 104:14–15 NLT

The homely plantain weed grows along many portions of my walking path. This plant is a rosette of ribbed, dark green, oval-shaped leaves, and the seeds cover several spikes that protrude from the center. It's not a showy plant, so it's easy to miss. However, the humble plantain weed is one of the most medicinally valuable plants in the area.

When I was the Bible study leader of a mommy group at church, I hosted a fellowship day at my house. One of the moms, a naturalist, became excited about the weedy patch of plantain weed near my driveway. She asked if she could harvest the leaves and seeds to make a natural diaper rash cream for our babies. I happily obliged her, and soon I had my own little jar of homemade ointment that worked to clear up skin problems for my youngest children.

Her creation inspired me to learn more about the usefulness of the plants and trees in my woods. I attended a class at the local nature center and learned I own a treasure trove of medicinally valuable plants on my property. Most of them are common weeds, yet few of them could compare to the versatility and usefulness of the plantain weed.

Plantain weed is edible—you can add it to soups, salads, stews, and stir-fries. You can steep the dried leaves for tea, infuse them into oils for topical applications, or add them into the natural lip balms and lotions you make. The seeds are used as a natural laxative. Studies suggest that plantain weed may reduce inflammation, improve digestion, and aid in wound healing.[1]

The more I learn about the usefulness of plantain weed, the more thankful I am for the great physician's healing powers in my life. It's easy to forget that most of the medicines I take are made from plants. They are in little capsules or white pills, looking nothing like the dark green leaves of plantain weed. However, those medicines I need from time to time are sourced from plants that God intended us to use for our good.

I love God's creativity in providing plants for our use. They are intended to feed us, strengthen us, heal us, and make us glad. The plants of summer are so abundant and beautiful, they fill me with joy. Whether I'm using them for food, strength, healing, or gladness, they wow me with the creative glory of our God. He created plants even before humans were made (Gen. 1:11), intending them to be for our nourishment and edification (Gen. 1:29). It is our job to subdue the plant world, to rein in its prolific growth for our good and God's glory (Gen. 1:28).

Among all the wildflowers, grasses, and leafy green trees of summer, humble plantain plants fade to the background. You will miss them unless you are looking for them. Yet they glorify God with their multiple capabilities. They seem to be intended mostly for our good. These plants are not showy, but they can help us in many ways if we harness their power.

Plantain weed now makes me smile. It reminds me that God is my healer, and he has graciously provided healing in the plants that grow right here on my prayer walk. He gives researchers, scientists, doctors, and pharmacists the wisdom on how to use certain plants for deep healing measures. God also helps regular people like me learn how to use plants in our own yards for healing and strength. We need to be like Adam and Eve in the first garden, continually curious and open to exploring the treasures of God's creation.

A few weeks ago, I gathered seeds from dozens of plantain plants in my yard. I stripped them from their spikes with a slide of my fingers and then scattered the seeds in a patch of the yard that is continually bare. I'm hoping and praying they will penetrate the clayey soil, set roots, and cover the bare ground with dark green rosettes. Even if I never make a tincture or salad from their oval leaves, it pleases me to know that the plantains are there, waiting to be used for my good. They remind me of God's abundant and glorious provision all around me, when I open my eyes and heart to see it. They'll grow right at the start of my prayer walk path, and they'll be nudging me to praise the great physician every day.

Prayer

Father God,

I praise you as my great physician. You know what I need for my physical, mental, emotional, and spiritual health. You are the source of all goodness in my life.

I confess that I sometimes doubt a cure or balm exists for my problems. It's tempting for me to choose the things of this world for soothing. Yet true healing and comfort only exist in your presence. I want to choose you first, when my hurt begins, so my health can be improved.

Thank you for providing many plants for our healing. Thank you for all the people you make wise so I can have products for better health. Thank you for the access to these materials, which make my life more comfortable and my pain more bearable.

Guide my decisions on which medicines to take, Lord. Provide for my healing when I am sick. May I never take my health for granted, but may I fully trust you as the healer of all my hurts.

In Jesus's name,
Amen.

Reflection Questions

1. Which pills, lotions, or ointments make your life easier?

2. What type of healing do you need now, and how can you seek this healing in the Lord's presence?

3. How are you inspired to praise God in new ways after reading this chapter?

NOTE

[1]Rachael Link, "What Is Plantain Weed, and How Do You Use It?" *Healthline*, June 10, 2020, https://www.healthline.com/nutrition/plantain-weed.

CHAPTER THIRTY

BICENTENNIAL

*But you will receive power when the Holy Spirit comes
on you; and you will be my witnesses in Jerusalem, and
in all Judea and Samaria, and to the ends of the earth.*

Acts 1:8 NIV

I am a proud fifth-generation resident of this area in the southeast corner of Missouri. Yet I must not get too attached to this area, and I must remember that I'm a part of the surrounding world too. It's tempting to walk the same prayer path, over and over, and to stay inwardly focused. However, God used the two hundredth birthday of Missouri in August 2021 to open my eyes to a broader picture, where problems have existed since its birth.

I got my ninth-grade nerd girl hat on one day to conduct research on the history of Missouri and revisit the same things I learned back in my high school US history class. The state of Missouri was created on August 10, 1821. It was formed under a compromise: Missouri would be admitted as a slave state, and Maine would be admitted as a free state. This was a political move intended to appease both slave owners and those promoting free-dom for slaves, since the votes between the groups would be equal in Congress.[1] However, historians say this appeasement move back-fired. It was one of the main factors that led to the Civil War forty years later.

My county is one of the first five formed in our state.[2] It has been one of the most prosperous counties in the area since that time. I'm not sure why we experienced such blessings compared to surrounding counties, but it likely had to do with the establishment of railroads and a teachers college in the late 1800s, which gave our county an economic and cultural advantage.[3]

One hundred miles to the north, riots broke out in Ferguson in August 2015 after Michael Brown was killed. A forty-five-minute drive to the south, Mississippi County struggles as one of the poorest counties in the whole state.[4] My county sits right between these hotspots for racial tensions.

The cultural shift in 2020 forced me to look at my surrounding region with new eyes. This is my Jerusalem, Judea, and Samaria, and I can't afford to ignore the truth about them any longer. I can't stay isolated in my economically blessed city on a hill and turn a blind eye to the needs of those in the surrounding areas. I need to be bolder about shining my light before the people I encounter anytime I leave my home, especially right here in my corner of the world. I need to listen, pray, and offer support. During Missouri's bicentennial month, these are the matters that peppered my prayers.

The problems in my area have deep roots that won't change overnight. But I believe in the power of prayer to change the world for the better. I know the problems begin in the hearts of people, and their hearts must change for problems to be solved. I am praying that God will change the hearts of the people in my Jerusalem (my county), Judea (surrounding counties), and Samaria (state of Missouri).

I regularly thank God for the blessings he has graciously bestowed on me here, because I don't want to take them for granted.

I also pray for God to give me greater insight into the problems and greater compassion for the people who suffer from things that feel foreign to me. On my prayer walks, I lay down my ignorance and resistance before him. I ask him to give me a humble, teachable heart that is willing to do whatever he calls me to do to change this region for the better. Then, when I step off the prayer walk route and out into the community, I'm better prepared to be the salt and light God wants me to be.

What a blessing it is to be an agent of the Holy Spirit in this area, two hundred years after my state was admitted to the union. What a responsibility and privilege I have to shine the light of the gospel message here in southeast Missouri, where five generations of my family have lived. I want to honor God in doing this more intentionally in the days to come. Praying about this on a regular basis keeps me mindful of my place in this time of history and my calling to be a wholehearted Christian right here where God ordained me to live.

Prayer

Father God,

I praise you for the place where I live. I praise you for the unique blessings you give me right here. I praise you for the opportunities I possess to be salt and light in my own community.

I confess that I often overlook the blessings I experience in this area. The freedoms and privileges are easy to overlook. It's also tempting for me to ignore the suffering of people in my region. But I want to make a difference, and I need you to help me do this, Lord.

Thank you for my Jerusalem, Judea, and Samaria. Thank you for calling me to be an agent of peace and love in all of these areas. Thank you for this age of the Internet when it is easier than ever to spread the gospel all around the world. May I take these responsibilities seriously, God.

Give me insight into the unique problems of my region. Guide me into how I can offer prayer, practical help, or financial support to the suffering in my area. Soften my heart to be humble and teachable so I am ready and willing to do whatever you call me to do in service to the people near me.

In Jesus's name,
Amen.

Reflection Questions

1. Where are your Jerusalem, Judea, and Samaria?

2. What problems do you know about these areas?

3. What specific types of help are you willing to give to the suffering people in your region?

NOTES

[1] "1821: Missouri Becomes the 24th State Admitted into the United States August 10, 1821," Missouri 2021, accessed November 1, 2021, https://missouri2021.org/ara-homepage/missouri-timeline/.

[2] "1812: A Portion of the Louisiana Territory Is Renamed the Territory of Missouri by Congress to Avoid Confusion with the New State of Louisiana," Missouri 2021, accessed November 2, 2021, https://missouri2021.org/ara-homepage/missouri-timeline/.

[3] Joshua Hartwig, "150 years later: Remembering Louis Houck, 'the Father of Southeast Missouri,'" *Southeast Missourian*, April 22, 2019, https://www.semissourian.com/story/2603309.html.

[4] "Mississippi County, Missouri," Wikipedia, accessed November 2, 2021, https://en.wikipedia.org/wiki/Mississippi_County%2C_Missouri.

CHAPTER THIRTY-ONE

MUSHROOMS

Everything on earth will worship you;
they will sing your praises,
shouting your name in glorious songs.

Psalm 66:4 NLT

In August 2020, unusual rains came into our area for several days at a time. This is normally when the hot, humid dog days of summer oppress our gardens and fields. Yet this unexpected moisture produced a flush of mushrooms in my woods and on the wooded roadsides of my prayer walks.

As you know, I don't usually take my phone along on my walks. But that month, I tucked it into the pocket of my shorts to capture photos of the mushrooms. They displayed God's glory in a dazzling array of shapes, sizes, and colors. I stooped down to snap photos of tiny specimens that lived only a day or two under the canopy of shade and rain clouds.

Their variety mesmerized me: little white caps with brown shingles, rubbery yellow-orange ruffles on a decaying branch, brown buttons with a black dusting, dusty orange ovals with white undersides, dark brown caps with flares like daisy petals, spooky white spore towers reaching upward like skeleton fingers, a tiny bright red mushroom just like a holly berry, coral pink caps with snow-white gills, a ridged yellow disc with a brown edge. I could describe dozens more, but this was the thrilling sample along the edges of my driveway.

I know that mushrooms grow from spores that stay in the ground, and different mushrooms grow on their decaying matter of choice. I also know that mushrooms love to grow in warm, damp, dark places, so they flourished like I had never seen before that August. The conditions were right for their beauty and diversity to be on display, even during quarantine. The abundant rains in an off-season activated their growth.

As I was admiring the mushrooms and pulling Memphis back so he wouldn't taste test them, I pondered these fungi facts. They reminded me that God is the master artist. He uses his heavenly paintbrush to create these wondrous designs, and it's obvious that he loves diversity. There's no doubting that the mushrooms were shouting God's name in glorious praises through their sizes, shapes, and colors. And if I am a masterpiece of God's creation, far superior in design to these beautiful fungi, how much more does he want me to sing his praises?

God had to work many factors together for the mushrooms to flourish that month: the best humidity levels and heat range, the right spores in the perfect locations, the exact amount of rain to coax fungi into flourishing in a season when they are normally dormant. In the same way, God hides inspiration waiting to be awakened by the right conditions in my life. Like hidden manna tucked away in a jar, God supernaturally preserves it to be opened and shared at the exact right time for his glory and my enjoyment.

On my prayer walks, I recounted the times I doubted God had preserved any manna for my nourishment: the many Augusts affected by stress, financial strain, unwanted transitions, and relationship struggles; times when I thought opportunities had completely dried up; seasons when I thought hope was not just dormant but dead.

I struggled with doubts in August 2020, when my children would have full-time online learning during quarantine. How would they flourish socially in the teen years when friendships are so important? How would they be impacted academically in the school years that are important for career foundations? These pressing matters had been on my mind and in my prayers.

But God, in his perfect timing and wonderful sense of humor, spoke hope to me through humble mushrooms. If they could not only grow but flourish in an unexpected season, my children would flourish despite the challenges they would face. God had rain stored up to awaken the hidden hopes and dreams in the woods of my heart. Through the mushrooms, he displayed his power to create new, vibrant life from death. Maybe something in me had to die too so that something more beautiful could be built upon it. Perhaps if I persisted in worshiping God every day, singing his praises and shouting his name on my prayer walks, I would discover the hidden manna for which I had stopped hoping.

That's exactly what happened. I can look back now, more than a year later, and see the good things God was growing in the darkness. I can now see the rains he brought at the right time to reactivate growth. If I had given up hope in early August 2020, I would have missed out on the blessing of discovering these truths today. The memory of the mushrooms reminds me not only to praise God for his artistry and timing, but to put my hope in him once more.

Prayer

Father God,

I praise you for the amazing diversity of creation. You love to create amazing things from your vast imagination. What a blessing it is to be named as the masterpiece of all your creation, Lord!

I confess that I have doubted you. When I thought my dreams were dead, and I gave up hoping and praying, I only saw the darkness. I couldn't see what you were working under the surface, waiting for the right conditions to revive.

Thank you for surprising me with blessings in unexpected seasons. Thank you for your sense of humor, which humbles and delights me. Thank you for the many lessons I can learn about your character from nature when I open my eyes to your truth.

Give me hope that you are working right now in ways I can't see, that you will awaken blessings for me when the conditions are right. May I trust you more each day as I wait for the rains to fall, and may I anticipate displays of your glory in my life with ever greater joy.

In Jesus's name,
Amen.

Reflection Questions

1. How have you seen God's glory and creativity in a surprising way?

2. When has God helped you grow and flourish in an unexpected season?

3. What blessing might God awaken in the right conditions for you?

AUTUMN

CHAPTER THIRTY-TWO

BLACK WALNUT

Blessed is the one who always trembles before God,
but whoever hardens their heart falls into trouble.

Proverbs 28:14 NIV

At several places along our walk, Memphis and I encounter black walnuts that have dropped on the path in the fall. These native Missouri nuts are encased in hard green shells, which we avoid stepping on. If the case has a single crack in it, the sticky black pulp inside will leave a permanent stain on my shoes. I dare not touch it with my fingers, or the stain will last for weeks. I'm pretty sure it's a main ingredient in my hair dye—that's how powerful it is.

Walnut trees produce beautiful wood. They have a dark, rich grain that's popular for use in furniture, cabinets, flooring, and gunstocks. The wood is dense and hard, durable and strong. It is naturally resistant to decay and insects due to a trait I'll soon describe.

The walnut trees on our path are mixed in with all the other trees: maples, oaks, hickories, ashes, and cedars. However, they secrete a unique substance known as juglone, which is toxic to many other plants and trees. For example, if you plant an apple tree near a walnut tree, the juglone will poison the apples with blight. It's also detrimental to pines, birches, and tomato plants.[1]

Once you're able to extract the walnuts from the shell, they don't taste mild like English walnuts. They have a distinctive flavor profile that usually polarizes people. I count myself among the lovers of this nut. I adore black walnuts in chocolate cookies at Christmastime, and they are delicious in homemade fudge and other sweets.

But getting the nuts out of the shells is a major undertaking. You can't use a simple nutcracker and metal pick like you would for pecans. My grandmother puts a flat piece of cardboard over the shells and then runs over them with the tractor. That's how much pressure is required to break off the messy shells. We've also put gloves and safety glasses on before breaking them open with hammers. The shells make it difficult to get to the good stuff. I've given up on this hard work and simply purchase them from locals who are willing to invest the effort. I buy their nuts already shelled for my brownies and cake recipes.

Everything about a black walnut tree is *hard*. Hard wood, hard shells, hard for other plants to get along with—it's an obnoxious neighbor that doesn't naturally grow in its own stand but mixes in with other trees, spreading its poison around. No one sees how beautiful the wood is until the tree topples.

When I spot the green walnut globes on my walk, I take time to pray for the most difficult people in my life, the people displaying the dark side of their personalities, which tear down rather than build up. Although I've taken time to learn their backstories to show compassion for their hurts, their abrasiveness still hurts. That's even more reason to commit them to prayer.

I keep their faces in my mind as I pour out my frustrations about these people. God is always gracious to listen to my stories of the anger, hurt, fear, and sense of injustice they have stirred up in me. He asks me, over and over, to vent my problems vertically so I do not grow hard and bitter inside.

Then I lift up prayers for God to replace their hearts of stone with hearts of flesh, to make them humble and teachable (Ezek. 36:26). I ask God to give them greater self-awareness before their pride causes them to fall (Prov. 16:18). I pray that they will learn from their troubles and gain humble spirits (Prov. 28:14).

Finally, I pray for my own attitude toward these black walnuts in my life. I pray I would learn what *not* to do and how *not* to treat others through their negative examples. I ask God to help me forgive and be willing to practice longsuffering. God has been kind to teach me about setting boundaries and sticking with them, to prevent my own fruit from being poisoned by their influence. I want to be known as one who loves these polarizing people, even if that's only possible through regular prayer.

After walking through this prayer sequence, I feel more at peace. I can't do anything to change the basic nature of the black walnuts in my life. Their hardness could be strength rather than a stumbling block. Their tenacity could be used to build something beautiful and long-lasting. Their fruit could be nourishing and enjoyable if it is set free for use. This is the hope I hold for the incredibly difficult people in my life. I pray that they will come to a full knowledge of the double-sided truth about themselves that's true of all of us: that they are beloved by a heavenly Father who longs for them to draw near, and that they are sinners desperately in need of the grace only he can provide.

Prayer

Father God,

I praise you for the opportunity to learn from negative examples. You always give me reasons to keep growing, and often the best learning comes through hard situations.

I confess that I do not always value these challenging lessons from people who are hard for me to handle. Their ways irritate me, and I want to withdraw, criticize, and lash out instead of practicing self-control around them.

Thank you for teaching me a different way, Jesus. You were patient even with the Pharisees, whose hard hearts eventually condemned you to die. You showed them respect they didn't deserve, and you never stopped longing for them to be saved. Thank you for your wonderful example of how to treat difficult people.

Help me heal from the hurts difficult people have inflicted on me. Remind me to vent vertically when I feel frustrated or angry. Teach me what not to do from their examples. Keep my heart from becoming hard against them. I want to be known as someone who loves difficult people well, and I need your constant guidance in how to do this.

In Jesus's name,
Amen.

Reflection Questions

1. Who is a black walnut in your life?

2. What have you learned from the negative examples of difficult people you've encountered?

3. How can the sequence of venting vertically, praying for others, and then praying for yourself help you deal with the most difficult situations in your life?

NOTE

[1]Research taken from: "Black Walnut Gunstock Blanks and More," The Lumber Shack, accessed October 21, 2021, https://www.thelumbershack.com /pages/information.

CHAPTER THIRTY-THREE

DUMP

He will delight in obeying the LORD.
He will not judge by appearance
nor make a decision based on hearsay.

Isaiah 11:3 NLT

I am not sure who regularly commits this act. One of my country neighbors dumps their food waste on a particular place of my prayer-walking path. I think it must only be one family committing this deed, because the dumping occurs in the exact same place every time. Their unauthorized dumping stomps on my nerves but has taught me to pray as well.

When you live in the county, you don't have automatic trash pickup like you do in town. You can pay for it through a service. We do this ourselves. It's not an outrageous expense—it's around twenty dollars per month. Some people choose this method, and others favor the old-fashioned way of using a burn barrel. The vapors from plastic waste in burn barrels are unsafe for the environment and toxic for breathing, so we don't use one. Yet several of our neighbors still use this method for trash disposal.

However, someone has decided to dump things like spoiled spaghetti, moldy pizza, stinky catfish skins, rotten deer carcasses, and smelly melon rinds on the side of the creek. This stuff would be fine in a burn barrel or perfect for bagged-up trash pickup. However, for reasons I don't understand, several times a month I deal with the putrid smells of this junk. I also deal with Memphis straining with all his 125-pound might to sniff and gobble this disgusting mess, if the circling vultures and crows have not yet consumed it.

I don't understand why these mystery neighbors handle their trash in this way. Do they not want to pay for pickup, or can they not afford it? Why do they not burn things right away in their burn barrel so raccoons won't be attracted to the messes overnight? I don't know who to ask to find the answers to these questions.

For a while, I fussed and fumed over this issue. *How dare they be so irresponsible,* my inner critic raged. *Don't they know any better? Isn't it a hassle to drive this yucky stuff over here? Wouldn't it be much easier to burn it or schedule pickup?* I ruminated on all the angles I could imagine.

Yet the only answer to which I confidently arrived was that my most characteristic sin—criticism—was alive and well. I didn't want to keep feeding this problem that rears its ugly head in me way too often. So, I begrudgingly began using the dumped mess as a prompt on my prayer walks.

I started out being honest with God about my negative feelings. I admitted that I flat-out don't agree with how these faceless yet real neighbors are handling their trash. Reluctantly, I set my reasonable points of contention to the side. Then I prayed about my own critical spirit. I imagined the shame these people would feel if they were found out and criticized to their faces. I didn't want to be the one to condemn them, so I handed this problem over to the only righteous judge, the Lord God Almighty, again and again on my prayer walks.

Walking by these messes did not produce good feelings in me. Yet, prayer walking by these messes produced growth in me. I need to be less critical and more prayerful for many people in my life, especially the ones whose faces I can see. Through this dumping ground prayer prompt, I get lots of practice in forgiveness, compassion, gentleness, and kindness behind the scenes before I deal with disagreeable people in person.

When I see cars and trucks pass me on the road, I wonder if the drivers are the ones who dump the messes. Is it the person with the loud muffler who must pause at the top of the hill before continuing, presumably because they need repairs they can't afford? Is it the truck driver from the family of five living in the shed who seem to be cash-strapped? Is it the elderly couple who drive at a fixed and frustrating twenty-five miles per hour? Instead of judging them, God has taught me to pray for their provision and peace so I can become more like Jesus.

Isaiah prophesied about Jesus's character eight hundred years before he was born. In part of his description in chapter 11, Isaiah says that Jesus will not be judgmental based on appearances or hearsay. He will take delight in obeying God rather than falling into these temptations. Because Jesus is this way, and because I follow him, I need to be more like that. I never thought oozing trash on the side of the road would teach me that lesson. But I know that my Father will use whatever he wants to shape me more to his Son's likeness. For this reason, I'm grateful for the dumped mess, although I still pinch my nose shut while praying.

Prayer

Father God,

I praise you for teaching me truth even in negative situations. You use whatever you want to get through to me, and sometimes it comes through a nasty surprise. I praise you for tucking valuable lessons into all the corners of my life.

I confess that I often jump to judge others before knowing the full situation. I criticize and condemn without practicing self-control, although I get defensive when others do this to me. Forgive me for sitting on the seat of judgment, which only you can occupy with full righteousness, Lord.

Thank you for tucking grace even into the most difficult situations of life. You want me to learn something from these negative lessons, and you will help me as I seek you. Thank you for being so kind as to work even the negative things of life for my good.

Help me delight in obeying you, focusing more on my spiritual growth than the sins of others. May the Holy Spirit prick my conscience when I am tempted to judge by appearance or make decisions based on hearsay. May I grow to be more Christlike in these issues.

In Jesus's name,
Amen.

Reflection Questions

1. When have you been tempted to judge someone without knowing all the facts?

2. Which unpleasant situation has God used to teach you a valuable lesson?

3. How is God using something unexpected to shape you to be more like Christ?

CHAPTER THIRTY-FOUR

NEIGHBORS
ON THE ROAD

Get rid of all bitterness, rage, anger, harsh words, and
slander, as well as all types of evil behavior. Instead,
be kind to each other, tenderhearted, forgiving one
another, just as God through Christ has forgiven you.

Ephesians 4:31–32 NLT

Occasionally, Memphis and I encounter other dogs on our walks, and I see their territorial nature on display every time. A fight nearly always ensues, and no one wins, especially the worst version of me who is yelling, yanking, and, I am sorry to say, sometimes kicking.

It's in a dog's nature to defend and protect his or her own territory. Memphis does not understand the common use of the country roads, and neither do Brucie or Remy, our neighbor's golden retrievers. Each dog thinks that the road is theirs and theirs alone to protect, and they growl, bare their teeth, bite, and wrestle to prove it. Although Memphis is on a leash and the other dogs are loose, all of them act as if they are in charge. Remy goes so far as to leap up and nip my shoulder to claim her queenly throne. I don't know what else to do except head back to my property as fast as possible, because my loud protests make no difference. I know the dogs don't understand, and I will never be able to reason with them. Instead, I must quickly head home to protect myself and keep Memphis from being injured. On those days when Brucie or Remy are outside, we simply walk laps around the cemetery at the church, far from their territorial gaze.

But Memphis is no different in terms of claiming territory. Even when we walk alone with no interference, he makes his marks. As soon as we head outside before a walk, he will empty what seems to be his full bladder. Then, anytime he stops to sniff a patch for more than five seconds, he pees on the area to claim his territory. His bladder capacity amazes me! Even on a long thirty-minute walk, he has plenty of liquid stored somewhere inside, laced with his unique scent, to mark the places he feels belong to him, although his markings extend far beyond my property lines.

Less often, we meet human neighbors on the gravel road. Sometimes a mom and child ride by on their horses, usually on Sunday afternoons. Another time, we met a lady on foot. Each time we have passed one another, they have remarked, "I thought this road belonged only to me," and we have politely laughed. I must admit, I feel the same way since I walk it so often. I know in my head that the road isn't mine, but when I'm on it, a territorial spirit stirs deep inside my sinful heart. The same one must have spoken out when I was a two-year-old: "Mine!"

The dogs and neighbors on the gravel road remind me to confess my territorial selfishness to God and open up my heart and mind to other perspectives. Oh, how often this territorial spirit stirs in my thoughts and feelings while driving, waiting in line, and other pop-up moments when I didn't see it coming. *Mine,*

mine, mine! it cries in a self-centered tone, although the actual space doesn't have my name on the title. Although the word never escapes my lips, sometimes the selfish tone leaks out in murmurs, sighs, huffs, and eye rolls.

That attitude is the root for the selfish behavior the apostle Paul describes in Ephesians 4:31. If I let it go all the way to its limits, it will manifest in those ugly ways. However, the Holy Spirit gently nudges me on my prayer walks to be kind, tenderhearted, compassionate, and forgiving in those tempting moments, because I have been forgiven countless times by Jesus, who suffered on my behalf. Out of my desire to obey him, I must surrender my selfish territorialism over to him and declare him the king of the world, who rightfully rules over every single jurisdiction.

Even the gravel road belongs to him. The county may have legal rights to it now, which no one else can claim. But in the spiritual sense, God is the owner, and he deeply desires for me to demonstrate a spirit of tenderhearted love to everyone on it. Whether that looks like picking another route to avoid a fight or kindly saying hello to fellow travelers, I am responsible for my attitude on the road. Thankfully, the Holy Spirit comes alongside me, empowering me to subdue the two-year-old territorial demands in my heart and put on the accommodating attitude Jesus always offered.

Prayer

Father God,

I praise you as king of the world. You rule with perfect justice and sovereignty over all situations. You own all things and sustain all life. We are simply your stewards, and you call us to live in harmony as a reflection of your glory.

I confess that I harbor selfishness and territorialism in my heart, God. It shows up in many ugly ways, through my attitudes and actions. I know these sins put barriers between me and others, as well as between you and me. Forgive me for erecting these sinful walls that promote division instead of harmony.

Thank you for calling me to be a kind, considerate, compassionate person. Thank you for empowering me to live this way through the power of your Holy Spirit. Left on my own, I'll fall back into my sinful ways and even make worse decisions. But with your help, I can be an agent for good in this divided world.

Show me the situations in which I have an attitude like a two-year-old. Give me the fruit of self-control as I choose to interact with others in harmony. May I follow Jesus's example of being tenderhearted, forgiving, and accommodating.

In Jesus's name,
Amen.

Reflection Questions

1. Which situations trigger a territorial spirit in you?

2. When you feel that two-year-old inside shouting *Mine!*, what steps can you take to get back on track for God's glory?

3. Which new acts of tenderhearted love are you willing to try this week?

CHAPTER THIRTY-FIVE

HERITAGE

For the LORD will not forsake his people;
he will not abandon his heritage;
for justice will return to the righteous,
and all the upright in heart will follow it.

Psalm 94:14–15 ESV

One September evening, my prayer walk extended up to the family farm. It's only a mile north of my house, and I needed to visit it for healing and hope.

That evening was rare in that I was all by myself. My former husband was out of town, and my children were spending the night at their grandparents' home. My grandma, who lives at the farm, was out of town too. It was an ideal time for me to get some grief out in the open, since no one but God and Memphis would be present to witness it.

Many Midwestern families have had to make tough decisions about their family farms. When no family member wants to care for the farm anymore or no one can afford to purchase it, the farm may go to auction. It is then either swallowed up by surrounding farmers or turned into residential areas, normally subdivisions with dozens of homes.

Our family farm faces a similar fate. I don't think any of the six children wish to purchase it outright. Once Grandma is gone, it might be divided into different farming parcels or perhaps converted into more residential spaces. The future for our family farm is uncertain.

As I extended my normal walk far beyond the bridge, I prayed around all the spaces where I walked. I offered thanksgiving for the good memories of my great-grandparents, who first purchased the farm in the 1950s. I thanked God as I passed by the place where the hog shed once stood, where I got to see the squealing piglets nurse from their fat mamas. I thanked him when I passed by the former site of the smokehouse, for all the provision of meat from this farm. I thanked him as I walked around the ponds, remembering delicious meals of fried catfish and bass, when so many of us gathered. Most of all, I thanked God for the faith they both displayed, which was passed on to me.

Then I began thanking him for the memories that started in the 1990s, when my grandparents moved from town to care for the farm and for my great-grandmother. While I walked by the living room wall, I thanked God for many wonderful Christmases, when my grandparents gave us each a Santa sack filled with treats. I walked by the front room and thanked God for all the times they babysat my children, forming strong and loving bonds with them. I walked by the kitchen and thanked God for many meals shared for the nourishment of our bodies and souls. I walked in the sleeping garden and thanked God for the year that my grandparents gave me a section of it to grow flowers, peppers, and pumpkins, which I watered and weeded while they cared for my oldest son, then only a toddler. I thanked God for their heritage of faith even in all the trials they had faced and for the many times they had encouraged me in my own.

I walked to the front fields where I could see the sun starting to lower in the sky. Tears streamed down my face as the memories kept rolling: so many summers of hay hauling, so many butchering days and fish fries, so many days of sewing with my great-grandmother and baking with my grandma, so many visits to stave off my loneliness as a young mom. I lifted my arms up, gratefully offering them back to the Lord, thanking him again and again for the heritage of faith so clearly felt on those 104 acres of farmland.

As I turned toward home and the evening darkened, my oldest fear—the fear of abandonment—rose in me. *Who will I be when the farm is no longer in the family?* I wondered. *I will be all alone again, just as I've always expected,* I thought. But the Lord wrapped his arms around me while I walked down the lane. He invited me to pour out my fears before him. He reminded me that he has promised to never leave me nor forsake me (Heb. 13:5b), and that promise will be just as true in the days to come as it is now.

Before walking back home on the gravel road, I stopped to visit the graves of my great-grandparents, right across the road. The tears began drying from my face as I imagined how happy they would be to see that I was living by faith and passing it on to the next generation. I thought about God's faithfulness in preserving a heritage of faith to me through them, and I renewed my trust in him. I know that anytime I need to process anticipatory grief, the grief to come, I can use a prayer walk to process it and be reminded of God's constant presence.

Prayer

Father God,

I praise you for preserving a heritage of faith for me. Whether it came from family, friends, or others, you kept the thread running through your people so it would reach me. What a gift to receive the faith that people fought to preserve over the centuries! What a treasure this is to me, Lord.

I confess that I sometimes get bogged down with grief. I don't handle it well, getting stuck in the stages of denial, bargaining, sadness, and anger. You want me to reach the final stage of acceptance by pouring out my grief to you. Forgive me for keeping it bottled inside.

Thank you for comforting me through prayer, Lord. Your ever-listening ear is a comfort for my soul. Thank you for good memories that teach me about your faithfulness to me.

Help me trust you not to abandon or forsake me, because I am your heritage. May I trust that you will bring justice and peace at the right time and that your plans will come to pass according to your will. May I be upright in heart, following you more closely day by day.

In Jesus's name,
Amen.

Reflection Questions

1. What is your heritage of faith?

2. What positive memories of your childhood bring you joy today?

3. How might regular prayer help you process a current area of grief?

CHAPTER THIRTY-SIX

BIGGER THAN ME

Now all glory to God, who is able, through his mighty power at work within us, to accomplish infinitely more than we might ask or think.

Ephesians 3:20 NLT

In autumn 2019, I nearly wore a rut in the gravel road, taking to it several times per day for prayer. That's when my first traditionally published book was set to release, and my anxiety rose high. But God used those prayer walks to calm and strengthen me when the challenge I faced seemed too big.

Since age thirteen, I have wanted to write books. I've kept journals since age ten and dreamed of seeing my name in print. I began blogging in 2010 and started self-publishing in 2016. Yet what I wanted most was to help as many people as possible through my writing, and I knew that traditional publishing is the best route for that dream. I had to work hard to make the necessary connections before signing with my agent and then signing my first book contract in May 2018.

I turned the manuscript in to the publisher in August 2018. Two months later, I traveled to Dallas, Texas, for a Lifeway women's event with my best friend. I had read books by most of the speakers, and I was looking forward to the worship and teachings. It was a great way to celebrate the hard work I had accomplished.

During the breaks, I sat in my seat high in the arena and watched the authors at their stations, signing books and taking photos with fans. A spirit of fear rose in me as I realized that, in less than one year, I would have my own traditionally published book to sign. I looked at the hundreds of women standing in line to get their books signed. Feeling overwhelmed by the task in front of me, I silently prayed, "I can't do this, God. It's too big for me."

The Lord answered me right there in my seat. In his loving, fatherly voice, he spoke to my heart, "You don't have to do it alone. I will help you do it." This moment was a great comfort to me in the months ahead and a balm for the spiritual warfare I had faced while writing the book.

As summer changed to autumn in 2019, I began building my launch team. The tasks were huge, even with the help of my launch team manager. I also faced unprecedented spiritual attacks that threatened my family. My anxiety kept rising as the publishing date of October 1 approached. The best way to deal with it was to take to the gravel road, sometimes two or three times a day, to pour my feelings out before the Lord.

I found myself saying again, "This is too big for me." Yet in prayer after prayer, I would follow up with God's own words to me: "But I know I don't have to do this alone. You will help me do it." I prayed over all the people helping me do it, including my launch team members, publisher, book distributors, delivery people, and future readers. Every day, I surrendered the giant matter over to God, and he was faithful to give me peace in exchange for my anxiety each time.

Looking back on that time, I'm glad I went on so many prayer walks. I'm grateful that God made the project bigger than me, because then it could accomplish far more than I could possibly ask or think. The project was bigger than me, but it wasn't bigger than God. He had plans to work his mighty power through me before I ever typed a single word.

I remember catching a glimpse of this power at work at my Barnes & Noble book signing. My friend from church brought her friend who was going through a marriage crisis. My friend had given her my book, and they brought it to the store for me to sign. The suffering woman leaned close to give me a hug. She whispered in my ear, "Your chapter on unforgiving thoughts has helped me forgive my husband." She said she almost didn't come to the bookstore that day because she wanted to stay home and keep reading it! After she left, I rejoiced with tears because God knew my book would help that woman release her pain. I praised him for his glory on display right in front of me.

My writing career is a frequent bigger-than-me topic on my prayer walks. Many other topics have fallen into that category. When I feel the overwhelm of a bigger-than-me situation, I know it's time to hit the gravel road and pray it out, surrendering it so I can experience God's peace. I also know that whether I see evidence or not, God will accomplish infinitely more than I can ask or think in the situation through his mighty power that he promises to work within me. He deserves all the glory for being bigger than me and doing far more through me than I can dream on my own.

Prayer

Father God,

I praise you for being so big, much bigger than me. This means you are in control, and I can trust you to handle every detail of my life.

I confess that I get overwhelmed by situations that are out of my control. I forget that I was never meant to handle them all on my own. Instead, you want me to trust you more as I surrender my problems to you. Forgive me for getting caught up in anxiety spirals rather than deepening my dependence on you.

Thank you for hearing every prayer I speak when I'm overwhelmed. Thank you for accepting every white flag of surrender I wave. Thank you for giving me your perfect peace in exchange for my anxiety, as often as I need to receive it.

Show me situations in which I need to surrender to you rather than trying to handle it on my own strength. Comfort me through the fact that you are bigger than me, and you can shoulder all the problems I throw on you. May my faith grow and may my peace increase as I pray each bigger-than-me prayer.

In Jesus's name,
Amen.

Reflection Questions

1. Which bigger-than-me situation have you seen God show up in?

2. Which bigger-than-me problem are you facing now?

3. How might daily surrenders of your problem to the Lord in prayer help you find greater peace?

CHAPTER THIRTY-SEVEN

WHITE OAK

*To all who mourn in Israel, he will give a crown of beauty for
ashes, a joyous blessing instead of mourning, festive praise
instead of despair. In their righteousness, they will be like
great oaks that the LORD has planted for his own glory.*

Isaiah 61:3 NLT

Right before we purchased our property from the church, they
cleared the most valuable trees from it, including the long-living
Quercus alba, also known as white oak. The wood is used for cabinets and interior trim and is famously used for whiskey barrels.[1]
The trees that were cleared from our woods were likely made into
such things.

We tried to convince the church to let us pay even more for
the property so we wouldn't have to deal with the leftover treetops. I also wanted to retain more of these beautiful trees on our
property. However, they were the rightful owners at the time, and
they proceeded with the clearing. It took us years to clean up all
the branches and dig out the stumps.

But the loggers were not able to remove one glorious white oak
from our property. It stands too close to the road, and it may have

damaged the asphalt if they had tried to move it. This majestic tree towers higher than any of the other trees, probably one hundred feet or more, and it may even be over one hundred years old. It is in its full glory during autumn, when its large green leaves turn to rich nutmeg brown, one side glossy and the other matte. Its plentiful acorns drop to the ground to feed deer, turkeys, raccoons, squirrels, and birds all winter long. If it had not grown so close to the road, the tree would have the broad, round, shady spread the most beautiful white oaks possess.

I view this tree's towering beauty each time I descend the hill toward the gravel road. I consider how many storms and droughts this tree has weathered, yet it still stands firm. It is unshaken by winter winds and unbothered by summer heat. Once a tiny acorn, this tree grew to great heights with God's care of rain, sunshine, nutrients, and protection.

I marvel at its testament to God's faithfulness in the times with which I am familiar. It did not topple in the terrible ice storms of 2008 and 2009, although we lost nearly half of our trees in those winters. The tree did not suffer unrecoverable loss during the summer droughts of the years that followed, when the leaves of corn curled inward to conserve moisture and farmers resorted to feeding their cattle dried cornstalks due to a hay shortage. It stood strong during the February 2017 tornado, which I am sure hovered over our property since I heard that signature freight train sound a few minutes before it touched down north of here. The tree has not died and turned into a snag for woodpeckers, which has been the fate of several of its peers. No, it has remained because God's hand has been upon it, just as his loving hand has been upon me.

When I look back on the years we've lived on this property, I see much sorrow and suffering. My former husband and I built our home to serve as a family hub, but so many relationships have broken since that time, that dream died. It has only been recently resurrected through our teenagers who host parties for their friends—a true joy for me, yet nothing like I imagined when we designed and constructed the living spaces.

The property was long a source of contention between my former husband and me, a cruel bargaining chip in our most heated arguments. He saw it as an asset to be sold, much like the spec houses he builds as his trade. I saw it as my fortress and even wrestled with idol worship of my home. This acreage was often an entry point for arguments that eventually ended our marriage.

There has been much heartache since we purchased the property in 2003, yet there has been much growth in me during that same period. It's as if God sent those struggles to make my faith as strong and tall as the white oak tree standing in our woods. I don't think I would be writing this book today if I hadn't suffered as much.

Through that tree, God shows me his majesty. He shows me his faithfulness. Then he invites me to accept his gifts: a crown of beauty and a joyous blessing in exchange for my sorrow. He wants me to give him festive praise for delivering me from all the suffering. I want to live a righteous life in thanks for all he has done. I want to be a great oak planted for the Lord's own glory, as beautiful, lasting, and fruitful as the white oak in its fall glory.

Prayer

Father God,

I praise you for your majesty. You are the Lord God Almighty, my constant source of strength and power. Your faithfulness is beyond comparison.

I confess that I lose sight of your strength and might in my life. I get caught up in the storms I face and look downward on my problems. I let my problems drag me down for too long, and my joy is too easily sapped. But I want to renew my hope and faith in your everlasting strength, Lord.

Thank you for standing strong with me through all the struggles I've faced. Thank you for promising to give me beauty, blessings, and reasons to praise in exchange for my ashes, mourning, and despair. Thank you for your comfort, goodness, and faithfulness to me.

Make my faith strong and sturdy through the trials I face. Help me reflect on how you have been faithful to me in the past to encourage me in my current struggles. May I be like a great oak planted to reflect your glory as I pursue a life of righteousness for your name's sake.

In Jesus's name,
Amen.

Reflection Questions

1. What person, place, or thing has been a constant in your life? How have you gained comfort or strength from this?

2. How has God made your faith stronger through the trials you have faced?

3. In which specific ways can you live a righteous life so you can be like a great oak planted for God's glory?

NOTE

[1]"White Oak," Missouri Department of Conservation, accessed November 2, 2021, https://mdc.mo.gov/discover-nature/field-guide/white-oak.

CHAPTER THIRTY-EIGHT

THE REDS

"Come now, let's settle this," says the LORD.
*"Though your sins are like scarlet, I will make
them as white as snow. Though they are red like
crimson, I will make them as white as wool."*

Isaiah 1:18 NLT

In July, a black gum tree hidden in a sea of green trees sends bright red leaves to my concrete patio, like gifts from heaven. The sight of these little red leaves whets my cravings for autumn, my favorite season of the year. The reds are my favorite leaves to see on my prayer walks in the fall.

My autumn woods are bursting with color in late October. The hard maples dominate the landscape with their golden yellow. Other trees like shagbark hickory, ash, black walnut, cork elm, redbud, tulip tree, and various oaks display fall leaves ranging from yellow to orange to brown. I like to play "I spy" for the rarer red leaves on my walks.

I took a couple of walks in our woods today before writing this chapter. They are at their peak color this first week of November, about two weeks later than normal. I rejoiced in finding so many of the reds. Depending on how the light fell through them in the morning or afternoon, I could see several shades among the different trees and shrubs.

To my left at the top of the driveway, I saw a few red leaves still holding onto the tops of the wild plum tree branches. This morning, I enjoyed the tart jelly I made from the abundant plum harvest in August, which turned out to have the same red shade as the fall leaves of the tree.

To my right at the top of the driveway, the dogwood trees have burgundy leaves that wink red when the sun shines through. I also notice red berries poking through the yellow-green leaves on my deciduous holly trees, and they will soon persist on bare branches, making a merry sight all winter. Even the dreaded poison ivy and poison sumac vines, which sent me to immediate care once during a nasty breakout, look pretty in shades of red as they climb tall trees.

Further down the hill, I visit the young sassafras tree. It's currently about ten feet high, filling out nicely in the full sun. I love the fun variety of its leaf shapes—mitten, oval, and trident. All of them are now mostly reddish, with speckles in many other colors. The red shines through most brightly when I see the afternoon sun behind them.

My favorite tree of all, sweet gum, grows tall on the far side of the levee. Its five-point star-shaped leaves are a rainbow delight of green, yellow, orange, purple, and red. I scan the tree with my eyes and spy the reddest ones about halfway up. Walking along the levee, I spot more black gum trees with their shiny oval red leaves. The smooth sumac at the edge of the pond has the most brilliant red leaves of all, and the bright pointed leaves transfix my gaze among all the golden shades.

On the way back home, I see elderberries holding on to purplish-red stems high above my head, where the birds will soon devour them. Even the purple leaves of the wild blackberry brambles look red with the afternoon light streaming through them. A plant called smartweed has many red stems with pink seed heads, and the stems seem to glow a soft red in the late afternoon light.

So many shades of red tucked among the abundant golds and browns—every red leaf, stem, or berry reminds me of the red I wore on Reformation Day at my former church. The color was a commemoration of Jesus's sacrifice. He shed his blood for me, and I must remember that I can only draw close to the Father, Son, and Holy Spirit because of Jesus's suffering and death.

My own sins bloodied him. Tears well in my eyes when I consider this fact. Every one of my sinful words, thoughts, and actions, intentional or unintentional, are reasons Jesus was beaten and tortured. He died for the sins of the whole world but would have done it all just for me. It's a fact I need to meditate on daily, and I do this through confession on my prayer walks.

Before Jesus came, the high priest made a special sacrifice once a year on behalf of all the people, in his foreshadowing of Jesus's sacrifice. He entered the Most Holy Place and sprinkled an animal's blood on the gold-covered Ark of the Covenant. This mysterious act satisfied God's requirement for a holy sacrifice to atone for the people's sins (see Lev. 16).

In my golden woods, I imagine myself sitting inside that holy wooden box—the one that held the hidden manna. All the gold surrounds me, and I don't deserve it. But as I see the flecks of red leaves in the sunlight, I watch God sprinkling Jesus's blood on me through the hole in the mercy seat. Through the veil of blood spatters, the Father sees me clean and white as freshly fallen snow, and he draws me near in love. All of this is because of Jesus, through him and for his glory. The reds bring me back into his throne room for grateful worship every autumn.

Prayer

Father God,

I praise you for the beauty of autumn. You didn't have to make this season so beautiful for us, but that's what you chose to do out of your grace and goodness. Thank you for the lavish displays of beauty you share with us in this season.

I confess that I often take my salvation for granted. I forget that Jesus suffered for each one of my sins. I need to remember his sacrifice daily to keep me humble and teachable, dependent on you for everyday grace. Help me to do this through daily confession, Lord.

Thank you, Father, for sending Jesus to die on my behalf. Thank you for covering me with his blood, so that when you see me, you don't look at my sins. Instead, you see me through the eyes of love, clean and whole in your sight, because of what he did for me.

Help me remember that I don't deserve your love, grace, or mercy. Yet you give it to me freely because Jesus sacrificed himself for me. May I never lose sight of this truth. May I ever be thankful for it and eager to share this truth with others that they may also be saved.

In Jesus's name,
Amen.

Reflection Questions

1. What do you enjoy most about autumn, and why?

2. What does Jesus's sacrifice mean to you personally?

3. Which sins do you need to remember that God has made white as snow thanks to what Jesus did for you?

CHAPTER THIRTY-NINE

BUCK

The Sovereign Lord is my strength!
He makes me as surefooted as a deer,
able to tread upon the heights.

Habakkuk 3:19 NLT

It seems like every November, when my boys leave to go hunt deer at the hunting property, I see deer right here on our property. They could have saved money and time by sitting on the porch deck to bag a choice doe or buck. However, Murphy's Law being in effect, if they did so, I doubt the deer would cross our levee or run through our woods that day.

One brisk November morning, the first Saturday of firearms season, Memphis and I went on our normal walk. I was bundled head to toe in all my cold gear, and I could see our breath as we walked down the hill. My mind was full of all the tasks on my to-do list, and I was ticking off prayer requests for each one. I was absorbed by the busyness that accompanies the weeks leading up to Christmas, and I wanted to get the prayer walk out of the way to tackle the rest of my tasks.

Without paying much attention to my surroundings, I kept Memphis clipping along with me, making good time. The faster pace also helped warm me up, and I moved my scarf down from over my mouth. The cold air felt fresh and clean in my lungs, and I heard the faraway booms from hunters' rifles.

Right as we came onto the crest of the hill, where the woods shade the gravel road, I saw a gorgeous eight-point buck less than twenty feet in front of us. He paused, I paused, and surprisingly, Memphis paused. Time seemed to hold still. All my concentration focused on this beautiful animal. I could hear his panting and saw his breath pluming from his nostrils. I noticed the condensation on his whiskers. The strength in his neck muscles and the power in his leg muscles was impressive. He held his perfectly symmetrical antlers proudly on his head and stood still one more moment, eyeing us with care. Once he determined we were not a threat, he made a huge leap over the road down the wooded hill and then bounded across the field toward the woods where I had seen several other whitetails go before.

Watching the buck reoriented everything for me. His masculine strength and beauty amazed me. His sure-footed leaps into rough terrain inspired me. He moved with such quiet power, I had to marvel at it. I slowed my pace to fully absorb the breathless moment.

As I reflected on what I had just seen, I praised God for many lessons he revealed, including his strength, power, beauty, majesty, and mystery displayed through the buck. I praised him for protecting and providing for all the wild animals around me, so many whom I never have the privilege of seeing. I praised God for bringing me on the path at the exact time the buck was crossing so I could see his glory up close. And I laughed with God, knowing that I had spotted the best deer of the day while my boys would probably come home empty-handed (that's exactly what happened, by the way).

God must love the wild animals so much. He helps a mother give birth to a healthy fawn and then provides for her nourishment as he grows. He gives a fawn spots to blend in with the dappled shade in order to protect him while his mother is away. He guides a young buck as he looks for food so he can grow strong and tall. God makes his antlers grow so he can compete in the social order and eventually impress a doe so the species is perpetuated. He must delight in helping the deer find cover again and again from all kinds of predators. He protects them in storms and keeps them warm in winter. There is much provision for so many animals, most of them never seen by humans.

Even more amazing to me, God promises to be my strength and make me as sure-footed as a deer. Although I do not tread upon the same heights as the buck I spotted on my prayer walk, I certainly face mountains of challenges for which I do not feel prepared or capable of handling. Yet God calls me higher and higher in my faith, and he prepares, guides, and strengthens me on my prayer walks. He wants my faith to grow, and he knows my growth requires strength to reach the higher places of maturity. As I pray, he strengthens my spiritual muscles in preparation for the challenges. I can look back and see how past prayers I uttered on the gravel road made my faith stronger. I know the prayers I will say in the days to come will connect me with the One who will strengthen me for greater heights in his sovereign love.

Prayer

Father God,

I praise you for your strength, power, beauty, majesty, and mystery. You sometimes stop me right in my tracks so I can praise these characteristics. How wonderful you are, Lord! How caring you are to provide so well for your wild animals and also for me.

I confess that I sometimes get so caught up in my to-do list that I don't take time to praise you for who you are. I don't stop to be still in your presence and marvel at your majesty. But when I do take time to do this, my faith is energized and refreshed. Help me make this choice more often so I can get to know you better.

Thank you for promising to make me as sure-footed as a deer, able to tread upon the heights. In the mountains I face, I need to cling to this promise. Thank you that as I rely on you for strength and guidance, you will make my paths more secure.

Remind me to be intentional in stopping to praise you daily. May I trust you more as I climb the mountains in my life. May my faith grow to new heights as I climb higher and higher toward you.

In Jesus's name,
Amen.

Reflection Questions

1. When have you had an up-close and personal experience with an animal? What did it teach you about God's character?

2. When is the best time of day for you to stop and marvel in awe of God?

3. Which mountains are you climbing right now? What steps can you take to rely on God's guidance and strength as you climb higher?

CHAPTER FORTY

SUNSET

*Those who live at the ends of the earth stand in
awe of your wonders. From where the sun rises
to where it sets, you inspire shouts of joy.*

Psalm 65:8 NLT

One of the few disadvantages to living in the woods is that I do not have a clear view of the sunset, one of my most treasured nature sightings. However, autumn evenings are the perfect time to head to a certain place on the gravel road where I can see gorgeous sunsets in full view.

Right after the time changes in November, I crave sun sightings more than ever. Since evening draws near between 5 and 6 p.m., I sometimes take a brisk walk with Memphis while supper simmers on the stove. We head out in the softening light, with the woods already half-dark. We need to walk past the bridge to see the sun on the western horizon.

Once we get to the bridge, we continue past the open field on the north that alternates between plantings of soybeans, corn, rye, and winter wheat. It is quiet this time of year after harvest is over and the birds and deer have picked the field clean of remnant seeds. Memphis and I walk up toward the church, on a steep hill that gets my blood pumping, and I can hear my heartbeat in my muffled ears. Then, we turn around at the top of the hill, catch our breath, and watch the glorious sun setting in the western sky.

The sunset view is always unique. Sometimes the sky is streaked with clouds that reflect the colorful rays. Other times the cloudless sky is a perfect ombre of blended colors. I can watch the colors shift right before my eyes, not unlike the Beyond Van Gogh exhibit I recently attended in St. Louis. However, this sight is more spectacular, more original, and more creative than even the best artists in the world can create since it's painted by the Creator himself.

As the sun drops lower, I can feel the temperature drop. I'll be chilled by the time I make it back home. Yet these few minutes of autumn sunset views are worth the sacrifice. They remind me God is with me at the close of each day. He is with me at the close of each season too, especially the challenging transition from fall to winter when my seasonal affective disorder flares. I chase the sun to cling to his promises to always be with me, and on the way home, praise overflows from my grateful heart.

It's important for me to get outside and worship God at all times of day, not just on sunny days that boost my mood, and not only when the wildflowers are in full bloom and the trees are in full leaf. It's good for me to get outside on these November evenings, when light is in ever shorter supply, tree branches are mostly bare, and wild animals are snug in their underground hibernation holes. I need to do this to praise God in every season, in every moment, even those which may feel less ideal. These moments when the light fades are perfect for inviting Jesus to walk beside me in my valleys, when night is falling and I feel alone.

He is with me in this literal valley, the gravel road between two hilly fields, low enough that I cannot see the setting sun anymore.

He is with me in the dark woods where I cannot see any possible threats. Beside me, he carries his rod and staff, not only to guide me but to ward off enemy attacks (Ps. 23:4). I trust that even in the darkness that deepens by the minute, he is preparing a feast for me in front of the evil rulers and authorities of Satan's dominion (Eph. 6:12) so that the cup of my heart will overflow with blessings (Ps. 23:5). That's why I am inspired to shout for joy even though it's almost too dark for me to see by the time I reach the top of the hill to walk down my driveway.

Season after season, God has been faithful to me on my prayer walks. He has hidden manna each morning, waiting for me to discover it. Whether the manna is in the sky, water, trees, flowers, animals, grasses, or even detritus strewn by people, I can find it when I seek for it with Spirit-led eyes. It feeds my soul, empowering me to grow a little more like Jesus every day.

I'm glad that my Memphis has been a faithful companion on these walks. He's heard all the prayers but never shares a word. I am certain he's also been amazed by God's goodness on our walks. I pray that someday, in the kingdom to come, God will allow me and Memphis to work alongside him in restoring this very road to its originally intended glory. That's a whispered prayer I often speak under my breath, just as the Earth turns on its axis one more degree and the sun slips down in the west. I can't wait to see it the next morning when I'll head out on the road again to collect more hidden manna on the country road.

Prayer

Father God,

I praise you for the gift of sunsets. How marvelous is your creative capacity, Lord! How beautiful you paint the evening sky, day after day, as a reminder of your faithful love for me.

I confess that I don't always seek the light in the darkness. I allow discouragement to get a foothold, and that's when the enemy of my soul does his dirty work. Forgive me for not turning to you immediately for help.

Thank you for promising to be right by my side in the changing seasons of my life and the valleys I face. Thank you for guiding and protecting me with your rod and staff. Thank you for preparing a feast for me in front of my spiritual enemies, proof that you have already won the victory over death and sorrow. Thank you for the joy you preserve for me.

Help me see the hidden manna all around me, whether on bright days or dark days. May these signs of your presence strengthen my faith and grow my love for you. May your Holy Spirit open my eyes to see more of these blessings hidden for my good in every season.

In Jesus's name,
Amen.

Reflection Questions

1. Where is your favorite place to watch the sunset?

2. How has God been your guide and protector in past valleys you've traveled?

3. What steps will you take to discover more hidden manna in your life?

ABOUT THE AUTHOR

Sarah Geringer is an author, editor, freelance writer, speaker, podcaster, artist, creative coach, and book launch manager. She is a member of the devotional writing teams for Proverbs 31 Ministries, Hope-Full Living, *Kingdom Edge Magazine*, and Woman 2 Woman Ministries. Her writing has also been featured on the *(in)courage* blog and at A Wife Like Me and Devotable.

Sarah holds a Bachelor of Arts in English from Covenant College and a Bachelor of Arts in graphic design and illustration from Southeast Missouri State University. She is a fifth-generation resident of southeast Missouri, where she lives with her three teens and two Labrador retrievers. You can follow Sarah as she writes and speaks about finding peace in God's Word at sarahgeringer. com, where you can also find color versions of the pictures in each chapter.

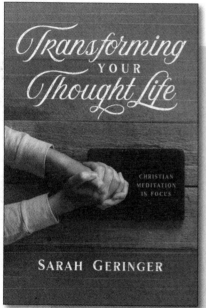

TRANSFORMING YOUR THOUGHT LIFE FOR TEENS

Renew Your Mind with God

ISBN 978-168426-221-2

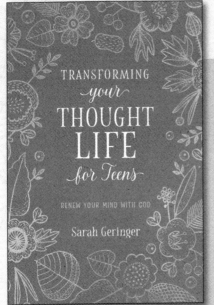

Every Teen Is Under Attack

Satan knows negative thoughts are the easiest way to tear a person down. It doesn't take many words to feel frustrated and defeated. To fight back, today's teens need strong minds, and the time-honored practice of Christian meditation can help them find victory in these spiritual battles.

Transforming Your Thought Life for Teens offers simple, guided meditations that can help your teen train their mind to stay grounded in God's Word. Each chapter examines a particular kind of negative thought pattern and provides key Bible verses and prayers for standing strong against it. Day by day, as your teen hides God's Word in their heart and mind, they will move closer to the heart and mind of God.

"Amazing book! Like a detailed map, this book leads teens out of the pits of unhealthy thinking and into the fields of freedom that come with a renewed mind! Sarah Geringer has created a biblically solid, wise, and authentic journey to help young women examine their thought lives. It's practical. It's inspirational. It's encouraging. Young women must be prepared for the life-long thought battle that will happen inside their heads. This book equips them to win."

—Heather Creekmore, author of *The Burden of Better*

1-877-816-4455 toll free
www.leafwoodpublishers.com

LEAFWOOD
PUBLISHERS
an imprint of Abilene Christian University Press